Advanced Introduction to International Tax Law, Second Edition

Elgar Advanced Introductions are stimulating and thoughtful introductions to major fields in the social sciences and law, expertly written by the world's leading scholars. Designed to be accessible yet rigorous, they offer concise and lucid surveys of the substantive and policy issues associated with discrete subject areas.

The aims of the series are two-fold: to pinpoint essential principles of a particular field, and to offer insights that stimulate critical thinking. By distilling the vast and often technical corpus of information on the subject into a concise and meaningful form, the books serve as accessible introductions for undergraduate and graduate students coming to the subject for the first time. Importantly, they also develop well-informed, nuanced critiques of the field that will challenge and extend the understanding of advanced students, scholars and policy-makers.

For a full list of titles in the series, please see the back of the book. Recent titles in the series include:

Comparative Constitutional Law
Second Edition
Mark Tushnet

Ecological Economics
Matthias Ruth

Freedom of Expression
Mark Tushnet

Private Law
Jan M. Smits

Globalisation
Jonathan Michie

Behavioral Economics
John F. Tomer

Environmental Impact Assessment
Angus Morrison-Saunders

National Innovation Systems
Cristina Chaminade, Bengt-Åke Lundvall and Shagufta Haneef

Private International Law and Procedure
Peter Hay

Law and Globalisation
Jaakko Husa

Regional Innovation Systems
Bjørn T. Asheim, Arne Isaksen and Michaela Trippl

International Political Economy
Second Edition
Benjamin J. Cohen

International Tax Law
Second Edition
Reuven S. Avi-Yonah

Advanced Introduction to

International Tax Law

Second Edition

REUVEN S. AVI-YONAH

Irwin I. Cohn Professor of Law, University of Michigan Law School, USA

Elgar Advanced Introductions

Cheltenham, UK • Northampton, MA, USA

Published by
Edward Elgar Publishing Limited
The Lypiatts
15 Lansdown Road
Cheltenham
Glos GL50 2JA
UK

Edward Elgar Publishing, Inc.
William Pratt House
9 Dewey Court
Northampton
Massachusetts 01060
USA

A catalogue record for this book
is available from the British Library

Library of Congress Control Number: 2018967818

ISBN 978 1 78897 848 4 (cased)
ISBN 978 1 78897 850 7 (paperback)
ISBN 978 1 78897 849 1 (eBook)

To Orli – You Are The Wind Beneath My Wings . . .

Thank you!

Contents

Acknowledgements

Several chapters have appeared in different form elsewhere and permission to include a revised version in this volume is gratefully acknowledged. Specifically, Chapter 10 is based on "Three Steps Forward, One Step Back? Reflections on 'Google Taxes' and the Destination-Based Corporate Tax", 2 *Nordic Tax J.* 1 (2016). Chapter 11 is based on "Evaluating BEPS" in Sergio Andre Rocha and Allison Christians (eds.), *Tax Sovereignty in the BEPS Era* (Kluwer, 2017), 97 (with H. Xu). Chapter 12 is based on "BEPS, ATAP and the New Tax Dialogue: A Transatlantic Competition?" 46 *Intertax* 885 (2018) (with G. Mazzoni). Chapter 13 is based on "Full Circle: The Single Tax Principle, BEPS, and the New US Model", 1 *Global Taxation* 12 (2016). Chapter 14 is based on "A Global Treaty Override? The New OECD Multilateral Tax Instrument and its Limits", 39 *Mich. J. Int'l L.* 155 (2018) (with H. Xu).

Abbreviations

ALS	Arm's length standard
AOA	Authorized OECD approach
APAs	Advance Pricing Agreements
ATAD	Anti-Tax Avoidance Directive
BEAT	Base erosion and anti-abuse tax
BEPS	Base Erosion and Profit Shifting
BPT	Branch Profit Tax of 1986 (US)
BIT	Bilateral investment treaty
CEN	Capital export neutrality
CbCR	Country-by-country reporting
CEO	chief executive officer
CFC	Controlled Foreign Corporation
CIN	Capital import neutrality
CON	Capital ownership neutrality
CIT	Corporate income tax
COGS	Cost of goods sold
CPM	Comparable Profits Method
CUP	Comparable uncontrolled price
CRS	Common Reporting Standard
CSA	Cost sharing agreement
ECJ	European Court of Justice
DPT	Diverted profits tax
E&P	Earnings and profit
EBIT	Earnings before interest and taxes
ES	Earnings Stripping Rule of 1989 (US)
EU	European Union
FATCA	Foreign Account Tax Compliance Act of 2010 (US)
FDAP	Fixed or determinable, annual or periodic
FDI	Foreign direct investment
FIF	Foreign Investment Funds
FDII	Foreign derived intangible income
FFI	Foreign financial institutions
FIRPTA	Foreign Investment in Real Property Tax Act of 1980 (US)

FTT	financial transaction taxes
FDII	Foreign derived intangible income
FFI	Foreign financial institutions
GDP	gross domestic product
GAAR	general anti-abuse rule
GILTI	Global Intangible Low-Taxed Income
IGA	Intergovernmental Agreements
IP	Intellectual property
IRC	Internal Revenue Code (US)
IRS	Internal Revenue Service (US)
ITAA	Income Tax Assessment Act
LOB	Limitation-on-benefits
MAAL	Multinational Anti-Tax Avoidance Law
MAATM	Multilateral Agreement on Administrative Assistance in Tax Matters
MFN	Most favored nation
MLI	Multilateral Convention to Implement Tax Treaty Related Measures to Prevent Base Erosion and Profit Shifting
MNE	Multinational enterprises
OECD	Organisation for Economic Co-operation and Development
PE	Permanent establishment
PFIC	Passive Foreign Investment Company
PPT	Principal purpose test
QBAI	Qualified business asset investment
R&D	research and development
SCM	Subsidies and Countervailing Measures Agreement
SEC	Securities and Exchange Commission (US)
TB	Trade or business
TNMM	Transactional Net Margin Method
TRA17	Tax Cuts and Jobs Act 2017
UT&FA	unitary taxation and formulary apportionment
UT	Unitary tax
VAT	value added tax

PART I

Overview of the international tax regime

1 Introduction: the international tax regime

In March 1923, four economists met in Geneva, Switzerland. They were there at the behest of the newly formed League of Nations to study the problem of double taxation. The report they prepared became the foundation stone of the international tax regime, and the principles they enunciated are today incorporated in over 3,000 bilateral tax treaties and in the international tax laws of the major economies of the world.

The main problem that the four economists (Professor Bruins from the Netherlands, Professor Einaudi from Italy, Professor Seligman from the United States (US) and Sir Josiah Stamp from the United Kingdom (UK)) set out to solve was the problem of double taxation. Countries are generally recognized to have the right to tax their residents on worldwide income "from whatever source derived", and also to tax non-residents on income arising within their borders. In the US, these principles are reflected in Internal Revenue Code (IRC) sections 1 (imposing tax on the worldwide income of residents) and 2(d) (limiting the section 1 tax in the case of non-residents to US-source income).

Already in the nineteenth century, it was recognized that this situation could easily lead to cross-border income being subject to taxation both by the country of residence and by the country of source. The issue of double taxation was the subject of several nineteenth century tax treaties. But the problem really came to the fore in the years following World War I, because the world was turning away from globalization with new tariffs and limits on immigration, and taxpayers became concerned that this turn would also be reflected in increased double taxation under the new high income tax rates enacted to finance the war effort. The result was an international financial conference held in Brussels in 1920 under the auspices of the newly formed International Chamber of Commerce, which called upon the League of Nations to address the question of double taxation. The report of the four economists was the result.

The economists were not chosen randomly. Two were from capital importing countries, Italy and the Netherlands, which traditionally supported source-based taxation and believed that residence countries should cede jurisdiction to tax-to-source countries. One was from the UK, historically the major capital exporting country, and believed that source countries should cede jurisdiction to residence countries. The fourth, Professor Edwin Seligman of Columbia University, was from a country that used to be capital importing but had recently become the world's largest exporter of capital. In addition, that country (the US) had in 1918 become the first in the world to adopt a foreign tax credit, which unilaterally gave precedence to the source country tax. Seligman was therefore well positioned to mediate between the others.

The resulting report first identified the problem and then made two major contributions toward a solution. The first was the "first bite at the apple" rule, which recognized that between residence and source the rights of the source country must prevail because, since the income arises within the source country, the residence country cannot prevent the source country from taxing that income. Thus, the economists wrote, the onus of preventing double taxation must fall on the residence country, and it can do so either by refraining from taxing foreign-source income (the exemption method, which a lot of European countries were practicing) or by granting a dollar-for-dollar reduction in its own taxes for the foreign tax paid, in other words, a US-style foreign tax credit (which at the time only the US had). What could not be permitted was for the residence country either to tax the foreign-source income of its residents in full, regardless of the source country tax, or to just grant a deduction for foreign taxes, because both of these methods result in double taxation (a higher tax burden on cross-border investment than on domestic investment).

The second major contribution of the four economists was to develop the benefits principle, under which active (business) income should be taxed primarily at source while passive (investment) income should be taxed primarily on a residence basis. The reasoning behind this compromise is now obsolete; nevertheless, that is the principle that underlies all the tax treaties, which maintain the right of the source country to tax active income while shifting the tax on passive income to the residence country.

By the time the first model treaty was drafted by a League of Nations Committee of Technical Experts in 1927, these two ideas had become well established and they are reflected in the treaty, which both puts the onus of preventing double taxation on the residence jurisdiction and shifts the right to tax passive income from the source to the residence country. The entire contemporary international tax regime is based on these principles, as well as on the single tax principle, which states that both double taxation and double non-taxation should be avoided. The single tax principle can be seen in the adoption by the US of the foreign tax credit, as well as in the work of the 1927 Committee on preventing tax evasion, but it was only fully developed in the post-World War II period, and it is still more controversial than the principles developed by the four economists. The Organisation for Economic Co-operation and Development (OECD)'s Base Erosion and Profit Shifting (BEPS) project from 2013 onward, as well as parts of recent tax reform in the US, are based on the single tax principle.

The single tax principle condemns both double taxation and double non-taxation. For residents, it indicates that the residence jurisdiction should tax income (whether active or passive) that is not taxed by the source jurisdiction under the "first bite at the apple" rule. For source jurisdictions, it suggests that withholding taxes should not be reduced unless it is clear that residence-based taxation will apply to passive income. The application of the single tax principle to residents was already established when the US rejected exemption as a way of relieving double taxation in favor of the foreign tax credit, because the main difference between these two ways of preventing double taxation is that a credit only applies if the source country taxes the income, whereas an exemption applies regardless of the source country tax. This is also why the US has consistently rejected "tax sparing", which is the granting of a credit even though there is no source country tax. The development of anti-deferral rules such as Foreign Investment Funds (FIF) and Controlled Foreign Corporation (CFC) rules by the US and other countries likewise reflects the single tax principle, because these rules attempt to tax on a residence basis income that is unlikely to be taxed at source because it is mobile. The recent adoption of a participation exemption for dividends paid to US parent corporations is arguably inconsistent with the single tax principle, but it is limited by many provisions intended to prevent double non-taxation, such as the exclusion of dividends treated as deductible interest by the source jurisdiction and the imposition of a minimum tax on most foreign source income.

The application of the single tax principle by source jurisdictions was implicit in the first model treaty from 1927, which included a withholding tax on interest that was refunded to the taxpayer upon showing that the income was declared to the residence jurisdiction. However, it took a long time for this side of the single tax principle to be widely adopted. Even the US reduced withholding taxes in treaties with purely territorial jurisdictions that did not tax foreign-source income (like France, with whom the US negotiated its first tax treaty in 1932), and also extended its treaties to tax havens like the Netherlands Antilles. However, in 1981 the US adopted as part of its first model tax treaty the limitation-on-benefits (LOB) article that limited reduction of withholding taxes to income that was taxed by the residence jurisdiction. At the same time the US terminated its treaties with tax havens and henceforth insisted on inserting LOB articles in every US tax treaty. The OECD ultimately adopted LOB as part of its commentary on its model tax treaty in the early twenty-first century, and the current BEPS project is explicitly based on adopting the single tax principle, at least in the treaty context. Thus, despite prominent exceptions that undermine the single tax principle, like the US portfolio interest exemption and "check-the-box" rule (discussed below), one can say that both the benefits principle and the single tax principle are now an established part of the international tax regime.

If one combines the benefits principle and the single tax principle, one gets a regime in which double taxation and double non-taxation are avoided by: (1) assigning to the source jurisdiction the right to tax active income and to the residence jurisdiction the right to tax passive income; and (2) allowing the other jurisdiction (residence for active, source for passive) to tax that income if the primary taxing jurisdiction refrains from taxing it. This should result in all income being taxed once: passive income at the residence jurisdiction rate (which varies from country to country based on the desired level of progressivity) and active income at the source jurisdiction rate (which tends to converge because it is mostly applied to corporations that are taxed at a flat rate, currently between 20 and 30 percent).

This regime makes sense because passive income is earned primarily by individuals, and in the case of individuals residence-based taxation is sensible because: (1) they cannot be in more than one place at once; (2) progressive taxation can meaningfully be applied to them based on the desired degree of equality; and (3) they vote. Active income is earned primarily by corporations and it should be taxed primarily on a source basis because corporations can be in many places at once;

corporate residence is not very meaningful; and neither progressivity nor voting applies to corporations.

The following chapters will describe the basic outline of the international tax regime in more detail. Chapter 2 will provide some definitions and discuss the two main types of jurisdiction to tax (residence and source). Chapter 3 will define the source of income and deductions that is crucial for taxing non-residents and for the foreign tax credit.

Chapters 4 and 5 will discuss the two main types of taxation of non-residents ("inbound" taxation). Chapter 4 will discuss inbound taxation of passive income and Chapter 5 will discuss inbound taxation of active income.

Chapter 6 will discuss transfer pricing, which is a variant of source-based taxation that applies to both inbound and outbound taxation, and that lies at the heart of modern efforts to tax corporations at source.

Chapters 7 and 8 will discuss "outbound" taxation, in other words, taxation of residents on foreign-source income. Chapter 7 will cover taxation of passive income and Chapter 8 taxation of active income. Chapter 9 will explain how all of the above gets modified when a tax treaty is in place.

2 Jurisdiction to tax and definitions

2.1 Jurisdiction to tax

In international law there are two generally accepted bases for jurisdiction, nationality and territoriality. A country has jurisdiction over its citizens regardless of where they are located because they have a personal link or allegiance to it. A country also has jurisdiction over persons or things within its territory.

In international tax law these two bases of jurisdiction have been transformed into residence and source jurisdiction. A country has the right to tax its residents (defined below) on their worldwide income. The reason that tax residence rather than nationality is used in this context is that otherwise it would be too easy for rich people to obtain a passport from a tax haven but live permanently in another country without being subject to worldwide tax anywhere.

A country also has the right to tax income that arises from sources within it. The concept of the source of income is difficult and will be discussed in the next chapter. Fundamentally, source is a legal rather than an economic concept, and is defined by source rules that are widely accepted for most types of income.

In theory, it could be possible to base taxation either purely on residence or purely on source. In a pure residence-based regime, each country would tax its residents on worldwide income, and no country would tax non-residents. However, most countries would like to tax non-residents, and in the case of corporations residence is not a meaningful enough concept on which to base the entire corporate tax. For these reasons source-based taxation is unlikely to disappear, despite the fact that modern economics tends to discount the concept of economic source.

Many countries used to base taxation only on source – in other words, to tax only income arising from sources within their borders – and were said to have pure "territorial" regimes. But with the advent of globalization and the relaxation of exchange controls in the 1980s, even countries that used to be purely territorial like France began taxing residents on worldwide income in some cases, in order to prevent wealthy taxpayers from escaping taxation by earning foreign-source income from mobile capital. The recent US tax reform did not result in the US adopting "territoriality"; it merely matched the participation exemption for certain dividends out of active income, while imposing a minimum tax on most foreign source income of US multinationals.

Thus, today we have, and for the foreseeable future we are likely to continue to see, countries applying both residence and source taxation simultaneously. This leads to the classic double taxation problem when a resident of one country earns income from sources in another, and both countries have the right to tax that income. The international tax regime arose from the attempt to solve this problem by giving the source country the primary right to tax the income but shifting the right to tax certain types of income to the residence country by treaty.

2.2   Defining residence

2.2.1   Individuals

In a world in which residents are taxed on worldwide income but non-residents are only taxed on income from sources within the taxing jurisdiction, it is necessary to define both residence and source. The source rules will be discussed in Chapter 3.

The definition of residence varies for individuals and for legal entities that are subject to income taxation, primarily corporations. For individuals, the common definition of tax residence depends on the fact that individuals can only be in one place at one time, and that generally travel across borders can be monitored by governments. Thus, the general definition of individual residence is based on counting days of physical presence in a given country. An individual who is physically present in a taxing jurisdiction for more than half a year, or 183 days, is considered a tax resident of that country.

Some countries exclude certain kinds of physical presence within a country, like that of students or medical tourists, but the general rule is that any day or fraction of a day counts. This definition makes it relatively easy not to be a tax resident in any country by avoiding physical presence therein (dividing your year among three countries typically means not being a tax resident in any of them).

Even if a person is a tax resident of a country, it may be possible to avoid being taxed on worldwide income by applying treaty tie-breaker rules. The definition of tax residence in tax treaties is based not on physical presence, but on a series of factors such as fiscal domicile (where your house and family are), habitual abode, nationality and the like. A person with a house in one country who is physically present most of the time in another risks being subject to worldwide taxation in both, but a tax treaty usually prevents this type of double taxation.

The US is unique in taxing its citizens on worldwide income even if they permanently reside elsewhere. This is a rule that dates to the American Civil War and is unlikely to be changed, but it causes many practical problems that have been exacerbated by the enactment of legislation (the Foreign Account Tax Compliance Act of 2010, or FATCA), designed to force banks to reveal the identity of American account holders directly to the Internal Revenue Service (IRS). It is far from clear how many US citizens live overseas and do not file tax returns; they may in some cases not even be aware that they are citizens (for example, if they were born in the US and left as infants). Nor does the US collect a lot of revenue from citizens living overseas, because they are usually covered by either an exemption for the first $100,000 of earned income or by the foreign tax credit. Law abiding citizens still file returns to get their US passports renewed and earn eligibility for social security (government pension) benefits, but others no doubt scoff the law.

Apart from the status-based taxation of citizens and permanent residents ("green card" holders) as residents regardless of where they actually reside, the US rules for establishing tax residency for individuals are rather typical. Any individual who is physically present in the US for 183 days in any given tax year is generally a US tax resident. However, in order to avoid situations in which individuals are present in the US for 364 consecutive days over two years without becoming residents, the US also counts days in the previous tax year as one-third of a day each and in the year before that as one-sixth of a day each. Days spent in the US as a student in an accredited educational institution, or as a medical tourist, do not count.

2.2.2   Corporations

There are two common ways to define corporate residency. The US rule is that a corporation is resident in the country in which it is incorporated as a legal matter. This makes it very easy to have a corporation controlled from the US count as a foreign corporation even if all its actual operations are in the US. In addition, the US in 1997 adopted a rule called "check-the-box" which permits US taxpayers to choose whether a foreign entity will be treated as a taxable corporation or as a non-taxable partnership or branch. It is therefore easy for US-based multinationals to avoid current taxation of foreign-source income by earning it through controlled subsidiaries incorporated in other countries, since the income is then treated as foreign-source income of a non-resident and therefore not subject to US tax until it is distributed as a dividend to the parent corporation. However, the 2017 US tax reform imposed a minimum tax requirement on most foreign-source income of US multinationals, as well as a one-time tax on their accumulated low-taxed foreign income.

Other countries tend to adopt a less formal definition of corporate residence based on the location of management and control of the corporation. This rule, which originated in the UK, can mean looking either at where the actual headquarters are or at more formal criteria such as where the Board of Directors meets. The latter interpretation makes it easy to have a non-resident corporation simply by having the Board meet in an airport hotel conference room once a year.

The combination of these two rules makes it relatively easy to have corporations that are not resident anywhere. For example, Apple's Irish subsidiary was incorporated in Ireland, but was managed and controlled from Apple's worldwide headquarters in Cupertino, California. This made it an Irish resident for US tax purposes and a US resident for Irish tax purposes, so that until 2017 neither country taxed it on worldwide income (which was almost all of its income). Currently, however, this income has been subjected to tax by the US, and the EU is also attempting to tax it under the state aid rules. Similarly, in the proposed Pfizer/AstraZeneca merger, the combined company was to be run in New York but incorporated in the UK, so that the UK would treat it as a US resident and the US treat it as a UK resident. Tax treaties do not really resolve this issue because they typically do not provide tie breakers for corporations. The Obama Administration proposed to adopt a "managed-and-controlled" test for at least some

US-based corporations, but this rule was not included in the 2017 tax reform, and in its absence, it is possible that transactions such as the Pfizer "inversion" may rise again to avoid the new US minimum tax.

3 The source rules

When the international tax regime was established in the 1920s and 1930s, economists believed that income had a naturally defined source. In general, they thought that active income (income from activities that the taxpayer controlled such as business income and wages) was sourced naturally to where the activity was conducted, while passive income (income from investments not controlled by the taxpayer) was sourced naturally where the capital was accumulated. This led to the benefits principle under which active income is taxed primarily at source and passive income primarily at residence.

Economists no longer believe that income has a naturally defined source, but source rules are needed as long as countries wish to tax non-residents. Thus, the source rules that were developed in the last century still apply as a legal matter, and they are incorporated by reference into the tax treaty network.

In general, source rules for income can be divided into two types: formal and substantive. Formal source rules are bright line rules that are under the control of the taxpayer, while substantive source rules seek to track the economic source of income. Most of the rules assign one source to each category of income even if economically it has more than one source.

In general, the formal source rules apply to passive income, because that income is supposed to be taxed primarily on a residence basis. The substantive source rules apply to active income because the source country has more of an interest in attributing this type of income to its economic source since it gets to tax it.

3.1   Formal source rules

The source rule for dividends is generally the residence of the payor, in other words, the corporation paying the dividends. This is a formal rule because it applies even if all the income of the payor derives from a source other than the country in which it is resident, so that economically the dividend does not originate from the country where the payor is resident. Given that the determination of the residence of the payor is generally under the control of the taxpayer under the rules described in Chapter 2, the source of dividends is also typically under taxpayer control.

The source rule for interest is the same as the source rule for dividends, in other words, residence of the payor. This is fortunate because it means that for sourcing purposes it is not necessary to distinguish debt from equity; but unfortunately the distinction needs to be made for other purposes described below.

The source rule for capital gains is the residence of the seller. This is strange because economically the source of capital gains should be the same as the source of dividends, since a capital gain is merely the value of current accumulated earnings plus the present value of future earnings. But for administrative reasons, it is hard to tax capital gains when stock is sold by one non-resident to another, while dividends can be taxed by withholding. Thus, it is understandable that capital gains are generally exempt from source-based taxation (unless they represent a large participation and the buyer wants to vote the shares, in which case a tax on the seller is enforceable).

3.2   Substantive source rules

The source of rents is generally where the real estate or other tangible property giving rise to the rent is located. The same rule applies to capital gains from the sale of real estate as it is easy in this case to locate the source and to enforce the tax, since the buyer would like to register ownership of the newly acquired property in its name.

The source of royalties is generally the country in which the underlying intellectual property is protected by copyright or patent law. This means that the source is where the intangible is exploited and not where it was developed, even though the costs of development were generally deductible in the country in which they were incurred. Some jurisdictions, however, source royalties to where the underlying intangible property was developed, leading to potential source-source double taxation.

The source of income from inventory sales of manufactured property is generally split between the location of manufacture and that of sale. This rule also applies to minerals and other commodities. The 2017 US tax reform amended this rule to source the income based on the location of production. However, the source of inventory purchased for resale is generally where title passes, which is now a formal rule because passage of title carries no economic consequences.

The source of services is where the services are performed. In the past, services typically were performed and consumed in the same country. Today, however, in the age of electronic communications, it is common for services to be performed in one country and consumed in another, a situation that currently raises questions about the viability of the traditional source rule.

3.3   The problem of sourcing

There are two major problems with the source rules. One is the lack of rules for many categories of income, such as alimony or cancellation of indebtedness. These issues are sometime resolved by countries enacting new rules, such as the US rule that income from derivatives is generally sourced to the residence of the recipient. This rule was adopted to protect the US derivative industry from withholding, but it is not accepted by other countries. In other cases, sourcing is done by analogy, for example, sourcing cancellation of indebtedness income to where interest would have been sourced had the borrower not defaulted. A classic US case illustrating this issue is *Korfund*, which involved a payment for a covenant not to compete from a US to a German corporation.[1] The German corporation argued that the source of the income was Germany because that was where the decision not to compete was made, but the US court held that the source was the US because that is where the income would have been earned had the covenant been breached.

---

1 *Korfund Co. Inc.* v. *Commissioner* 1 TC 1180 (1943).

A more serious issue arises when countries disagree on the characterization of income. Since the category determines the source rule and the source rule determines the right to tax this can result in double taxation. Some classic US cases can be used to illustrate this problem. In *Wodehouse*, the famous British comic author sold his rights to publish future stories in the US market to a US publisher for a lump sum payment.[2] The taxpayer argued this was a capital gain sourced to his location as the seller, but the US Supreme Court held that it was a royalty sourced to the place of use, because any stream of payments could be converted to a single lump sum payment. A third option, not raised by either side, was that the payment was for Wodehouse's services (sourced where performed). In *Karrer*, a Nobel-prize winning Swiss chemist entered into a contract with a Swiss pharmaceutical corporation to conduct research in exchange for a percentage of the US sales of the resulting patented product.[3] The IRS argued that this was a royalty sourced to the US, but Karrer argued successfully that the contract was for services performed in Switzerland. In *Boulez*, the musician traveled to the US to conduct an orchestra for a percentage of the sales of the recording.[4] Boulez argued the payment was a royalty exempt under the Germany–US tax treaty, but the IRS argued successfully that the payment was for services performed in the US. In this case, the German tax authorities disagreed and Boulez was taxed twice; the treaty was unavailing because the foreign tax credit does not apply to domestic source income and the competent authorities could not agree on the proper characterization.

It would in theory be better to have a uniform source rule for active income and another for passive income. For example, active income (from sales, services or royalties) could be sourced to where the buyer or consumer was located (similar to the current rule for royalties) because that would maximize source-based taxation of active income under the benefits principle, while passive income could be sourced to where it was deducted by the payor (an administrable rule designed to enforce the single tax principle). However, since the currently used categorization is built into existing treaties, this seems unlikely to happen.

---

2 *Commissioner v. Wodehouse* 337 US 369 (1949).
3 *Karrer v. United States* 138 Ct. Cl. 385 (Ct. Cl. 1957).
4 *Boulez v. Commissioner* 83 TC 584 (1984).

3.4   Sourcing deductions

Deductions are generally sourced by allocating them to the category of income they produce and then, as necessary, apportioning the deductions between foreign and domestic source income based on the applicable facts. For example, the salary of a chief executive officer (CEO) might be allocated to all of the firm's income, and then apportioned between foreign and domestic income based on how much of that income arose from foreign versus domestic sources.

This method can lead to similar problems of categorization as the sourcing of income, because it is ultimately based on the income sourcing rules. For example, in *Black and Decker* the US multinational set up a subsidiary in Japan in order to compete with its Japanese rivals on their home turf.[5] The venture failed and Black and Decker sought a worthless stock deduction. The company argued the source of the deduction was the US because it entered the venture to protect its home turf, but the courts held that the source was Japan because that would have been the source of dividends had the venture been successful. However, it could also be argued that the source in that case would be the US because Black and Decker could have sold the subsidiary, producing a capital gain sourced to the residence of the seller.

There are two common exceptions to this rule. Research and development (R&D) expenses are sometimes sourced to where they are incurred even if they generate foreign-source income, because a country might desire to encourage domestic R&D. In general, all taxpayers would like to maximize foreign-source income; residents because it increases the foreign tax credit or the amount of exempt income and non-residents because they are not taxed on foreign-source income. Conversely, it is always better to have domestic deductions. In the US, R&D is sourced half to where it is conducted and half to where the income or sales it produces are from, resulting in a significant tax subsidy to US-based R&D in cases in which all the R&D is in the US and all the sales are foreign (which would have resulted in 100 percent allocation to foreign income under the general rule).

Interest is sometimes allocated by formula, for example, based on the locations of a taxpayer's assets, on the theory that money is fungible. Other countries allocate interest by tracing it to the use of the funds,

---

5 *Black & Decker Co.* v. *Commissioner* TC Memo 1991-557 (1991).

or based on where the loan is booked. The US rule has undergone several changes. Before 1986, it was possible to locate all of a US-based multinational's borrowing in a single US finance subsidiary that would hold as its only asset notes from the US parent, resulting in 100 percent allocation of the interest expense to US assets. This was stopped by requiring consolidation of assets in 1986, but the consolidation was purely domestic, so that borrowing by foreign subsidiaries was allocated to foreign income but borrowing in the US was also partially allocated to foreign income. This rule resulted in too much interest allocation to foreign income and too little foreign income for foreign tax credit limitation purposes. In 2004, the rule was amended effectively to include foreign subsidiaries in the consolidation, resulting in a truly asset-based allocation, but this amendment has still not been fully implemented because of revenue considerations, even after the 2017 US tax reform.

4 Inbound taxation: passive income

The main distinction between taxation of residents and non-residents is that while residents may be taxed on worldwide income, non-residents as a jurisdictional and practical matter can only be taxed on income from sources within the taxing jurisdiction. Initially, non-residents were taxed on domestic source income in the same way as residents, in other words, on a net basis, although the tax was from the beginning enforced by withholding on payments at source. However, it soon became obvious that it was difficult for tax authorities to audit deductions of non-residents who had no business presence in the taxing jurisdiction. Therefore, since the 1930s, non-residents who receive passive income have been taxed on a gross basis, by withholding, and this tax is a final tax with no deductions allowed. For purposes of the foreign tax credit, it is treated as a tax imposed "in lieu of" the income tax on residents. This enables the withholding tax to be credited even though it is not an income tax since it does not allow for deductions.

4.1   The general rule

The scope of the withholding tax on non-residents is in general quite broad. Under US law, the tax is imposed on "fixed or determinable, annual or periodic" (FDAP) income from sources within the US (defined under the rules set out in Chapter 2). While originally the definition of FDAP was intended to limit the scope of the tax, court decisions have determined that "fixed or determinable" means determinable in hindsight (when the payment is made), even though the amount of the income could not have been determined before the transaction was completed. In *Barba*, for example, a Mexican national who won in a Las Vegas casino contested the withholding tax imposed on him on the ground that he could not have anticipated any winning gamble and in fact lost more on other bets.[1] The court, however,

---

1 *Barba* v. *United States* 2 Cl. Ct 674 (1983).

used the hindsight rule to justify the tax. Thus, gambling winnings can constitute FDAP even though one might not consider them "fixed or determinable" in the ordinary sense of those words. In addition, court decisions like *Wodehouse* have determined that even a single lump sum payment can be FDAP despite the reference to "annual or periodic". Thus, the modern definition of FDAP is quite broad: any payment from sources within the taxing jurisdiction that is not capital gains (which generally are excluded from FDAP under the source rules) generally constitutes FDAP subject to withholding.

The rate of withholding tax around the world tends to be quite high. In the US the rate is 30 percent, and it has remained unchanged since World War II, even though the net tax rate that applies to domestic taxpayers and to active income of non-residents has gone down from 94 percent in 1944 to as low as 28 percent in 1986. Under today's rate of 37 percent, it is frequently worthwhile for non-residents to organize their US investments as a trade or business, rather than a passive investment, in order to be subject to the regularly applied tax rate on net income rather than a withholding tax of as much as 30 percent, applied to gross income. However, this assumes that the 30 percent tax actually applies, and as we shall see below there are frequently exceptions that result in a much lower rate or even no withholding tax.

Nevertheless, it is accurate to say that the taxation of passive income at source is low in absolute terms; for example, the US collects about $4 billion per year in withholding tax on almost $2 trillion of annual inbound portfolio investment. The reason is that numerous exceptions swallow the general withholding rule. Most importantly, as discussed further below, interest on portfolio investments (in other words, investments by persons with only small ownership interests in the issuer of a debt security) typically are exempted from withholding tax. This exemption is consistent with the benefits principle under which passive income is supposed to be taxed primarily on a residence basis, but it raises some issues in regard to residence-based taxation of such income, which are discussed below.

4.2   The exceptions in general

The exceptions to withholding are numerous.

The first exception applies to capital gains, which are generally not subject to tax at source because they are sourced to the residence of the seller. This is justified on administrability grounds because it is hard for a source jurisdiction to collect tax on a sale from one foreigner to another. Nevertheless, many countries do subject sales of large participations to tax at source, because in those cases the buyer wants to vote the shares and the tax can be enforced by monitoring the registration of the stock in the buyer's name. For the same reason, capital gains on real property are frequently taxed because the buyer wants title to the underlying property. But capital gains on portfolio stock are typically exempt, and this is an important exception because economically the capital gain derives from the same underlying earnings as a dividend. The current European experiment with financial transaction taxes (FTT) may reveal something on the administrability of taxes on portfolio capital gains because the FTT is imposed on sales of portfolio stock regardless of the location of the sale. If the European Union (EU) can sustain the FTT on sales of portfolio stock in EU resident companies executed in, for example, New York, then it may be time to reconsider the general exception of capital gains from source-based taxation.

The most important exception from withholding applies to interest. In 1984, the US unilaterally abolished withholding on portfolio interest, and since then no large country has been able to maintain such taxes on interest paid to non-residents because the underlying investments would soon flow to the US. The EU savings directive, which was adopted in 2003, does not apply to interest to non-Europeans. As we will discuss below, this situation has led to significant problems with taxation of passive income of residents. In addition, the existence of a portfolio interest exemption but not a portfolio dividend exemption means that it is necessary to distinguish debt from equity, even though the source rule for interest and dividends is the same, and this can be quite difficult to do given modern financial instruments.

Royalties, which are an increasingly important category of FDAP given the importance of intellectual property to modern multinationals, are often exempted from withholding tax by treaty. In general, as discussed in Chapter 9, a main purpose of tax treaties is to reduce source taxation of passive income, and the OECD model treaty provides for no withholding on royalties. The ability of investors from non-treaty countries to benefit from this rule depends on the strictness of the LOB provision in the applicable treaty, and this varies by country. However, even in the US, which invented the LOB, it is frequently possible to achieve zero withholding by utilizing favorable treaties like that with the Netherlands. For example, in *SDI* a Netherlands Antilles company owned software which it licensed to its Netherlands parent, which in turn sub-licensed it to a US subsidiary for exploitation in the US market.[2] The royalty from the US to the Netherlands was protected by the treaty, and the LOB clause did not apply because SDI was a publicly traded company. The IRS argued that the royalty from the Netherlands to the Antilles should be treated as US source because it derived from the US to Netherlands royalty, but the court rejected this argument because it could have led to cascading taxation of the same income had the US to Netherlands royalty not been protected by the treaty.

This leaves dividends as the only major category of passive income subject to withholding. For several reasons, however, withholding taxes on dividends tend to be mitigated in practice. First, as mentioned above it is possible to transmute equity to debt by using derivatives, convertible shares, and other financial instruments, and in that case the interest is tax free. Second, the modern treaty trend is to reduce direct dividend withholding to zero even though the recipient is typically not taxable on the dividend under participation exemptions (including the participation exemption enacted by the US in 2017). Finally, derivatives such as total return equity swaps can mimic dividends in ways that are not subject to withholding, and, even though the US Congress took steps to restrict this exception in 2010, there are ways around this provision (which treats dividend equivalents as dividends) as well. For example, the new provision only applies to "notional principal contracts", a technical term that can be avoided. In other cases payments on derivatives are exempt because they are sourced to the residence of the recipient or because they are "other income" that is not subject to withholding under Article 21 of OECD-style treaties.

Thus, overall, it can be said that in most OECD countries there is very little actual withholding on FDAP. Arguably, this is as it should be under the benefits principle, and one might as well abolish withholding altogether since it raises little revenue at significant administrative cost. However, withholding may be needed to enforce residence-based taxation of passive income.

---

2   *SDI Netherlands BV* v. *Commissioner* 107 TC 161 (1996).

4.3   The problem of distinguishing residents from non-residents

In recent years, it has become clear that the abolition of withholding on FDAP of non-residents has made it possible for residents to pretend to be non-residents and benefit from the lack of withholding and information reporting, since most of the reductions are not treaty based and therefore no information exchange is possible.

This situation came to the fore in the wake of the UBS scandal in the US, when it was revealed that US residents were aided by UBS to set up corporations in tax havens and then invest funds belonging to these corporations through UBS back into the US. As a result, the US Congress enacted FATCA in 2010, which requires foreign financial institutions to report the identities of any US residents and citizens that have accounts with them directly to the IRS. FATCA in turn led to the development of both a network of bilateral intergovernmental agreements (IGAs) to provide for the reciprocal exchange of such information, and to dozens of countries signing onto an OECD sponsored Multilateral Agreement on Administrative Assistance in Tax Matters (MAATM), which provides for automatic exchange of information. Currently, the Common Reporting Standard (CRS) developed in the wake of FATCA has been adopted by over 100 countries (but, ironically, not the US).

It remains to be seen whether FATCA, the IGAs, or the MAATM/CRS will actually enable countries to tax their residents on worldwide passive income in the absence of withholding. I tend to be skeptical, because all these efforts depend on cooperation from numerous countries and financial institutions; a single holdout can undermine the whole system by attracting investors and providing secrecy. I would instead argue for coordinated refundable withholding taxes on passive income by the major jurisdictions, because funds have to be invested in them to bear a reasonable rate of return. The withholding tax has to be coordinated to prevent funds from fleeing elsewhere, but only by a few jurisdictions (the G20), and it can be made refundable upon showing that the income was declared to the country of residence, as envisaged by the original 1927 League of Nations model tax treaty.

5   Inbound taxation: active income

Active (business) income is supposed to be taxed at source based on the benefits principle. However, from the 1930s it became clear that some minimal threshold of presence in the source jurisdiction is required to justify source-based taxation, because otherwise isolated sales into a country could subject a taxpayer to the costs of preparing and filing a tax return, which in that situation could exceed the income from the transaction.

Thus, from the mid-1930s on, two thresholds generally have been used. Under a country's statutory law, where no treaty is applicable, the threshold is whether the taxpayer has a trade or business (TB) in the taxing jurisdiction. Where a treaty applies, the threshold is whether the taxpayer has a permanent establishment (PE) in the taxing jurisdiction. In general, the PE threshold is higher than the TB threshold. Both, however, require a physical presence (directly or through an agent) in the source jurisdiction, and in the age of electronic commerce this rule may pose a significant impediment to source-based taxation of active income. This is why the EU is currently debating replacing the PE threshold with a "digital PE" for corporations engaged in electronic commerce.

In addition, because a taxpayer that has a TB or PE in a source country can be audited, a question arises whether in that situation all of the taxpayer's income from that country, including passive income (which ordinarily would be taxed on a gross-income basis under withholding tax rules), should be taxed on a net basis. There is some disagreement on this issue, with the United Nations (UN) model treaty permitting passive income to be "attracted" to a PE while the OECD model rejects the "force of attraction" rule.

Two key questions tend to be most important in practice, under the rules governing either TBs or PEs. First, it is necessary to determine whether the taxpayer has a TB (if no treaty is in place) or a PE (if a treaty applies). Second, if the taxpayer does have either a TB or a PE, it is necessary to determine how much income is "effectively connected to" the TB or "attributable to" the PE.

5.1   Defining a TB or PE

A TB generally requires a physical presence in the source country, either directly or through a dependent agent (but an agent who is independent of the taxpayer legally and economically – sometimes a difficult factual test to apply – will generally not be a TB). In addition, under US law, a safe harbor provides that a taxpayer who invests on its own behalf in securities or commodities will generally not have a TB in the US. This rule was enacted when the US net rates were very high and deterred investors who were worried about subjecting FDAP to those rates with few deductions. For example, in *Chang Hsiao Liang* the taxpayer, who was a warlord in China during the 1930s, used an agent to invest funds in the US, and the IRS argued that the volume of the agent's activity made it a US TB.[1] The court rejected this view, but the risk of subjecting investment income to tax rates that exceeded 90 percent must have deterred other investors, leading to the enactment of the safe harbor in 1966. However, today the rules enable even some taxpayers who have a PE in the US to escape US tax because they lack a TB. This is particularly significant where the residence country exempts income attributable to a PE (on the reasonable assumption that it will be taxed at source), because double non-taxation is the result.

Beyond this, the definition of TB is not clear. A single apartment that is rented out with all costs falling on the tenant is generally not a TB, but two apartments may be. In *Lewenhaupt*, for example, a foreign taxpayer was held to have a US TB because he bought and sold several pieces of land through an agent.[2] On the other hand, a radio station broadcasting from Mexico into the US and deriving all its revenues from English language advertising in the US was held not to have a TB because it lacked the required physical presence in the US, and this set an important precedent for the age of electronic commerce.

A PE, in addition to the physical presence requirement, must also be engaged in the core activities of the business. Auxiliary activities such

---

1 *Liang* v. *Commissioner* 23 TC 1040 (1955).
2 *Lewenhaupt* v. *Commissioner* 20 TC 151 (1953).

as storage and even R&D will generally not give rise to a PE. However, the presence of an employee or dependent agent will generally be a PE if the employee or agent exercises authority to conclude contracts.

In recent years, a lot of attention has been paid to dependent-agent PEs. In general, controlling a subsidiary corporation in a source jurisdiction will not constitute a PE, but if the parent controls the daily activities of the subsidiary, there may be an agency PE. In addition, merely providing services can give rise to a PE in some circumstances, and the UN model treaty now envisages a "services PE". Some countries have held a server to be a PE even without people being present, and the same applies to a satellite node. The determination whether the requisite level of dependency exists can be difficult, as illustrated by the *Taisei* case, in which a group of Japanese insurance companies used a US reinsurer, and the IRS argued that even though they had no formal control over the reinsurer, agreement among them meant that as a group they had the requisite economic control.[3] The court rejected this argument after an extensive analysis, but this and similar cases illustrate that it is not enough to establish formal independence for the agent.

5.2   Attribution of income

For countries that reject force of attraction, the key issue is frequently not whether there is a TB or PE, but how much income to attribute to it.

Under domestic US law, there are two tests to determine whether income is effectively connected to a TB. If either the assets or the business activities of the TB generate the income, the income is effectively connected. This test generally makes it easy to render even FDAP into effectively connected income subject to net rates, which is useful for FDAP subject to the full 30 percent withholding tax since the net corporate rate is typically only 21 percent (plus any applicable state taxes).

The OECD has recently adopted the "authorized OECD approach" (AOA) to the attribution of profits to PEs. Under the AOA, the question should be determined by treating the PE as if it were a subsidiary

---

3 *Taisei Fire & Marine Ins. Co. v. Commissioner* 104 TC 535 (1995).

and determining its profits under the same arm's length standard used for transfer pricing (see Chapter 6). However, many countries have not adopted the AOA in actual treaties.

5.3   Special rules

There are three special situations where countries have adopted rules that differ from the normal operation of the active/passive distinction: real estate, branch profits and thin capitalization. In addition, the US in 2017 adopted a broad Base Erosion Anti-Abuse (BEAT) provision that is significantly tougher than a thin capitalization rule.

5.3.1   Real estate

Rents from real property generally constitute FDAP subject to withholding taxes. However, because there are significant deductions associated with owning real property, many countries give taxpayers the option to be taxed on a net basis.

Capital gains from the sale of real property (including mineral deposits) are frequently taxed at source because the tax can be enforced by blocking the transfer of the deed to the property. The same rule frequently applies to capital gains on the sale of stock in corporations deriving most of their value from real property. The tax is enforced by requiring the buyer to transmit an arbitrary percentage of the sale price to the tax authorities as a way of forcing the seller to file a return showing the actual gain or loss.

5.3.2   Branch profits

While dividends are generally subject to withholding tax as FDAP, remittances from branches (PEs) to head offices usually are not because they are made within the same legal entity. To equate the two situations, some countries (such as the US) have put in place a branch profit tax that applies to deemed dividend amounts from branches to head offices, at the same rate as the rate on an actual direct dividend.

5.3.3   Thin capitalization

One way of avoiding source-based taxation of active income is to capitalize a subsidiary or PE with debt rather than equity and use the interest deduction to reduce the source country effective tax rate. Therefore, most countries restrict the ability to deduct interest if the payer of the interest has a ratio of debt to equity above a specified threshold. In 2017 the US adopted a broad rule restricting interest deductions (both domestically and cross-border) to 30 percent of earnings before interest and taxes (EBIT).

The special regimes governing real property income, branch profits and thin capitalization can raise the question of discrimination under the tax treaties since they only apply to foreigners. However, the non-discrimination rule of the treaties is not usually enforceable by taxpayers, unlike the situation in the EU where the European Court of Justice (ECJ) has struck down thin capitalization rules as discriminatory. It can be argued that no real discrimination is involved since a foreign taxpayer that may or may not be taxable on a residence basis is not comparable to a taxable domestic entity.

5.3.4   The BEAT

In 2017, the US adopted the BEAT, which generally applies to all deductible payments (interest, royalties, and payments other than the cost of goods sold) from a US party to a related foreign party. The BEAT is an alternative minimum tax: the US party calculates its regular tax liability with the affected deductions at 21 percent, and then has to recalculate the tax liability without the affected deductions at the BEAT rate of 10 percent, and pay whichever result is higher. No foreign tax credits are available in the US against BEAT liability since it is a US tax on US source income, and other countries may deny foreign tax credits for the BEAT if they object to its legitimacy.

The BEAT has been criticized as violating the tax treaties. It can be argued that it is an indirect way of imposing a withholding tax on interest, royalties, and other income in violations of Articles 11, 12 and 21 of the treaties. However, since the BEAT is imposed on the US party, the savings clause – Article 1(4), found in all US treaties and stating that the treaty cannot generally affect US taxation of US residents – protects it.

Arguably, the BEAT is a violation of the non-discrimination provision (Article 24) since it only applies to payments to foreign parties, and the savings clause does not apply to Article 24. However, the BEAT applies regardless of whether the payment is from a US subsidiary to a foreign parent or a US parent to a foreign subsidiary, so in that sense it is not discriminatory. Moreover, even if the BEAT were found to be discriminatory, it could not be successfully challenged in court since it is a treaty override.

It remains to be seen whether other countries choose to retaliate against the US for adopting the BEAT, or whether they copy it as an effective way of protecting the domestic corporate tax base.

6   Transfer pricing

Under the benefits principle active income is supposed to be taxed primarily at source. However, as we saw in Chapter 2, the determination of the source of income is difficult and frequently under the control of the taxpayer. The issue becomes even more complicated when the task is to allocate income and deductions among members of a group of related corporations. Modern multinationals usually operate through a structure in which the parent company controls directly or indirectly hundreds of subsidiaries, and taxable income needs to be divided among them. That is the task of transfer pricing.

In theory, it is possible to treat the entire multinational as a single entity and either tax it on a consolidated basis (with the parent paying the entire tax but with a credit for foreign taxes on the subsidiaries) or apportion the group's income among different jurisdictions by a formula, which essentially ignores the separate status of the various corporations within the group. The first way was briefly used by the US in 1921–24, and the second (formulary apportionment) is used by US states and Canadian provinces for intra-national purposes, and has been proposed for internal use within the EU. However, since 1924 the dominant method of allocating income among members of a corporate group has been to treat each company as a separate taxpayer and to determine the correct transfer prices for sales of goods or services among the group members on the basis of the arm's length standard (ALS). The ALS, which is embodied in every tax treaty, states that the division of income among companies within a commonly controlled group should be based on estimates of how the income would be divided if the commonly controlled companies were instead unrelated companies, acting with respect to one another at arm's length.

6.1   The transfer pricing problem

The transfer pricing problem can be illustrated with the following simple example. Parent Corporation P owns 100 percent of a single subsidiary S. P manufactures widgets at a cost of 20 and sells them to S, which incurs distribution costs of 20. S sells the widgets to unrelated customers for 100.

If P and S were in the same country, they would file a consolidated return showing net profit of $100 - 20 - 20 = 60$, which would all be taxed in that country. But when P and S are in two different countries with different tax rates, the allocation of taxable income between the two countries depends on x, the price at which P sells the widgets to S.

Assuming neither party wants to operate at a loss, there is a continuum of possible prices x between the minimum acceptable to P, 20, and the maximum acceptable to S, 80. If P's tax rate is higher than S's, the parties would set x at 20. P would show profit of $20 - 20 = 0$, and S would show profit of $100 - 20 - 20 = 60$. If S's tax rate is higher, the parties would set x at 80. P would show profit of $80 - 20 = 60$ and S would show profit of $100 - 20 - 80 = 0$. Since the parties have to set x at some value, and since they are economically indifferent to x since ultimately the entire profit belongs to the P shareholders regardless of whether it is in P or S, even a small differential in the effective tax rate can lead to a costless shift of the entire 60 of profit from P to S or vice versa.

The challenge of transfer pricing enforcement is to prevent this shift happening. This, it turns out, is easier said than done, as the last 60 years of attempts to enforce the ALS have shown. The difficulty is illustrated by cases like *Dupont*, in which the US chemical company set up a Swiss subsidiary to acquire products from the US parent and resell them to marketing subsidiaries in high-tax European countries.[1] Even though an internal memo revealed that the Swiss company had no purpose other than tax reduction, it took the IRS over 20 years of litigation to win the case, and that case (ultimately decided in 1979) was the last unequivocal IRS victory in the transfer pricing area. Recently, however, there have been signs that the courts are beginning to shift in favor of the IRS.

---

1 *EI Dupont de Nemours & Co.* v. *Commissioner* 221 Ct. Cl. 333 (1979).

6.2   The classical methods and their limitations

Until 1968, laws did not attempt to provide detailed guidance for applying the ALS, and courts used their best judgement as to reasonableness to police transfer pricing. In 1968, the US adopted transfer pricing regulations with the three "classical" methods, and these were adopted by the OECD in its Transfer Pricing Guidelines in 1977.

The three classical methods are comparable uncontrolled price (CUP), cost plus, and resale price. Under CUP, the transaction between the related parties is compared to a transaction in the same good or service in the same market under similar conditions between unrelated parties. If such a transaction can be found, x is adjusted to the price charged in the comparable transaction.

Cost plus and resale price look at either the manufacturer or the distributor, assign a profit margin to it based on a comparison with similar manufacturers or distributors dealing with unrelated parties, and then set x to match that profit margin.

All three classical methods require a strict standard of comparability. However, the litigated transfer pricing cases in the period between 1968 and 1995 showed that courts either applied CUP based on inappropriate comparables which differed from the controlled transaction in some key feature, or rejected all comparables and used their best judgement as before 1968. For example, in *US Steel* the taxpayer used a Panamanian subsidiary to ship steel from Venezuela to the US, and was able to use the prices charged by that subsidiary to unrelated parties as a CUP, even though both the volume of shipments and the risk that the contract would be terminated clearly differentiated between the related and unrelated transactions.[2] Similarly, in *Bausch & Lomb* the taxpayer transferred know-how that enabled it to manufacture contact lenses at a much lower cost than its competitors to an Irish affiliate, and then successfully used the market prices for the lenses to establish the CUP, disregarding the cost differential.[3]

Eventually it became clear that the classical methods usually do not work because comparables cannot be found. Economists have argued that comparables cannot be found because of the economic

---

2 *United States Steel Co.* v. *Commissioner* 617 F2d 942 (2nd Cir 1980).
3 *Bausch & Lomb Inc.* v. *Commissioner* 92 TC 525 (1989).

circumstances which cause multinationals to form. It is usually cheaper and easier to deal with independent distributors in foreign countries, so if instead a corporation sets up or acquires a foreign subsidiary, the reason is that they are avoiding some costs that would be incurred if they dealt at arm's length. The most common example is protection of intellectual property (IP), which might be lost if divulged to an unrelated distributor. The net result is that in particular industries, especially those characterized by wide geographic spread and large size, it is simply inefficient to engage in business through networks of unrelated companies; all of the transactions within these industries occur among commonly owned members of multinational groups. Accordingly, close comparables from transactions between unrelated companies tend not to exist.

Ultimately, this realization led the US and the OECD to adopt in 1995 two new methods that are supposed to be based on lower standards of comparability.

6.3   The profit-based methods

The two new methods are the Comparable Profits Method (CPM) or Transactional Net Margin Method (TNMM), and Profit Split. They now have the same status as the classical methods and the taxpayer and revenue authorities are supposed to use whichever of the five methods requires the fewest adjustments (the "best method rule") and document it at the time of the transaction to avoid potential penalties.

Under CPM/TNMM, comparables typically are drawn from companies that are not in the same industry as the taxpayer under consideration, but arguably are from reasonably similar industries. The theory is that these margins typically will exhibit a bell-shaped curve. The bottom 25 percent and top 25 percent of the curve are eliminated and the profit of the tested party is checked. If it falls within the remaining middle 50 percent of profits, it is immune from further challenge.

This method was developed for use by tax administrators who have access to all of a country's tax returns. However, in practice it is a boon to the Big Four accounting firms, which perform the required comparables searches using financial data assembled from Securities and Exchange Commission (SEC) documents and other securities-law filings. Transfer pricing economists are charged with constructing documentation of the transfer price by choosing a sample of companies whose profits result in the tested company's profits falling within the middle 50 percent. For this the Big Four charge a hefty fee that is out of reach for small taxpayers.

In practice, under CPM and TNMM, the comparables found are often in widely different industries from that of the taxpayer under consideration, and the number of claimed comparables found is too small to support a statistically useful bell curve. The arm's-length ranges computed typically are much too large to be of great help in tax administration.

An alternative available method is Profit Split, which does not require so many comparables. Under Profit Split the functions of the related parties are analyzed and a standard market-based return is assigned to each based on publicly available data. Any residual, which represents the extra profit earned by the multinational, is assigned under US law to the developer or developers of the group's intangibles since it is presumed that IP is responsible for the residual. However, the OECD does not accept this particular description of the Profit Split method and does not offer guidance on how to allocate the residual.

6.4 The future of transfer pricing

There are numerous indications that even with the new methods, the economic error underlying the arm's-length theory has not been overcome, and transfer pricing rules are not working effectively. Before the 2017 tax reform, US multinationals had close to $3 trillion located in low-tax jurisdictions where they have little real activity. These profits were shifted despite transfer pricing enforcement.

A major culprit is cost sharing, a special method that allows profits to be shifted to subsidiaries that shared in the costs of developing IP. The theory is that because R&D has uncertain outcomes, cost sharing is risky for the taxpayer because if the project fails the deduction for the R&D is lost. But in practice multinationals only enter into cost sharing when they believe a project will be successful, and even if they are wrong, the lost deductions pale in comparison with the tax saved from shifting the profits.

Another problem area is Advance Pricing Agreements (APAs), which were supposed to save litigation costs (which can be very substantial

– large transfer pricing cases consume a disproportionate amount of resources). But many companies refuse to enter into APAs because taxpayers have won most decided transfer pricing cases since 1980, and even when APAs are concluded they remain secret, giving rise to the perception that multinationals can enter into hidden deals with the tax authorities.

In theory, applying unitary taxation and formulary apportionment would appear likely to yield a much more administrable and enforceable system, but for now the OECD, like many multinational companies, remains opposed to giving serious practical evaluation to formulary approaches even as it confronts BEPS. For example, the OECD rejected using a formula to allocate residuals within the Profit Split method, even though by definition residuals arise where there are no comparables and therefore the result of applying the formula is compatible with the ALS (since in the absence of comparables it cannot be proven that parties operating at arm's length would have split the profit differently).

Thus, in the foreseeable future, transfer pricing problems will remain, and solutions to the massive double non-taxation permitted under current rules are more likely to come from residence-based taxation of corporate groups, despite the uneasy nature of corporate residency determinations.

7 Outbound taxation: passive income

A US person owns 100 percent of the shares of a foreign corporation. The corporation earns foreign-source income (for example, from importing purchased goods into the US with title passing offshore). The corporation has no assets or employees – it is a pure shell – and all decisions are made by the shareholder who is also the CEO and the Board of Directors. What is the tax result?

Generally, the surprising answer is no current US tax. US tax law generally does not "pierce the corporate veil" by ignoring the separateness of a corporation, even if it is a shell. Establishing corporate status is easy under today's "check-the-box" entity-classification rules, which generally allow taxpayers to elect whether an entity is to have corporate or pass-through treatment; and establishing foreign status even easier since any corporation incorporated out of the US is foreign. Attempts by the IRS to attribute income to the shareholder have generally failed both under transfer pricing and under judicial doctrines like assignment of income, substance over form, economic substance, or sham. As long as the shareholder is careful about documenting the sales as made through the corporation the shareholder is safe, even though no actual business is done by the corporation (the goods are shipped directly from the supplier to the US, without passing through the tax haven that the corporation would typically be located in).

To be sure, what is achieved here is, under the US worldwide approach to taxation, deferral, not exemption. The individual US shareholder will be taxed if the corporation distributes a dividend or the shareholder sells the shares, and the only way out (if the shareholder is an individual) is to die since heirs can sell the shares with no income tax liability (before 2008, it was also possible to give up US citizenship, move, and live off the accumulated earnings, but that avenue of converting deferral to exemption was closed in 2008). But deferral, if it lasts for a long time, can be virtually as valuable as exemption because of the time value of money. Moreover, if the US shareholder is a corporation, then under the participation exemption enacted in 2017 for 10 percent shareholders, there will generally be no US tax even upon distribution of a dividend from the foreign corporation.

If the same scenario happened in the UK, arguably the result would be different because of the managed-and-controlled test for corporate residence, although in many jurisdictions this just boils down to having the Board meet offshore.

Because deferral (or exemption, in those countries that exempt dividends from foreign subsidiaries through a participation exemption, including the US) is easy to achieve, there are two types of anti-deferral/exemption provisions that are designed to ensure residence-based taxation of passive income: FIF and CFC rules.

7.1   FIF rules

There are two kinds of FIFs. The first is "incorporated pocketbooks" that a taxpayer controls to earn passive income (dividends, interest, royalties, capital gains) offshore. The second is a FIF in which the taxpayer is a passive investor and which he or she does not control.

The "incorporated pocketbook" is typically defined as a foreign corporation controlled by five or fewer domestic individuals whose income is mostly passive. The solution is either to ignore its existence or to have a deemed dividend of its income (all or just passive) to the shareholders. A deemed dividend is possible because the shareholders control the "pocketbook" and can distribute a dividend whenever they want to.

The non-controlled FIF presents a harder problem because the lack of control means that the shareholder may not be able to know what the income of the FIF is, and certainly cannot force a dividend distribution. This type of FIF is simply defined as a foreign corporation with a high level of passive income and/or assets generating passive income, with no control requirement. Under the US Passive Foreign Investment Company (PFIC) rules, the solution is to give the shareholder a choice of three methods of taxation:

(1) If the PFIC consents, it can let the shareholder know how much passive income it has and the shareholder declares the income on

its tax return; this is typically possible when US shareholders form the majority or a large minority in a FIF.

(2) If the FIF is publicly traded, shareholders can opt to be taxed on the rise in value of the shares as a proxy for the underlying income, but this carries the risk of not getting a refund if the stock declines.

(3) The most common alternative is an interest charge regime: when the shareholder receives a distribution from the PFIC or sells PFIC shares, the dividend or gain is spread backward to the shareholder's holding period and an interest charge is added to the tax amount based on the (fluctuating) interest rate on tax underpayment and the (changing) top individual tax rate.

FIF rules give rise to many problems. For example, holding companies may be FIFs even if the companies they control are active, and absent a look-through rule the FIF rules will apply. Another example is start-ups, which may be FIFs in their early years of operations because their only income is investment income.

In general, FIF rules are tough on paper, but the big question is compliance: the residence country tax authority needs to know that the FIF exists and that the resident individual owns shares in it, which subjects the tax administration to the same information issuer as those discussed for inbound passive investment in Chapter 4.

7.2   CFC rules

The US was the first country to adopt CFC legislation, called "Subpart F", in 1962. The basic characteristics of US CFC legislation are the following:

(1) It requires over 50 percent control to designate a foreign corporation as a "CFC". In order to be counted, each shareholder must have at least a 10 percent share in the foreign corporation.

(2) It follows a transactional approach according to which the rules apply to foreign companies wherever they are located (so the CFC rules also apply to foreign companies that are not located in tax havens).

(3) The income earned by the CFC is treated as deemed dividend only if it can be classified as tainted income, which is passive

income (that is, primarily, with certain exceptions, dividends, interest, capital gains and royalties), base company income (that is, income arising from transactions between companies within the same group) and 956 income (generally, loans of the subsidiary companies to the shareholders). From 2018 on, tainted income also includes Global Intangible Low-Taxed Income (GILTI), discussed below.

Because of the effects of globalization and the free movement of capital, many countries faced the same problem of the movement of income to zero- and low-tax affiliates of multinational groups. The US approach to taxing CFCs, as a way to limit tax deferral, was widely followed by many jurisdictions, including purely territorial jurisdictions (where the consequence of income shifting is exemption rather than deferral): Germany (1972), Canada (1975), Japan (1978), France (1980), the UK (1984) and over 20 other countries since then. Despite the significant degree of convergence in CFC legislations, on a more detailed level, significant differences persist even for countries that have adopted CFC rules (and most countries do not have them yet), although all EU member countries are bound to adopt them by 2019

As a result of the wide adoption of CFC rules, the distinction between global and territorial jurisdictions has lost much of its importance. On one hand, territorial jurisdictions seek to tax passive income earned by their residents from foreign sources through the operation of the CFC rules, and many have endorsed worldwide taxation of individuals. On the other hand, global jurisdictions tend to allow deferral for active income earned by their residents through CFCs, and the recent trend has been to go even further and exempt dividends distributed by CFCs to their parents. This was always the rule in territorial jurisdictions (the so-called "participation exemption"), but it has been adopted by global jurisdictions such as the UK, Japan, and now also the US.

Four major structural variables serve to distinguish between CFC regimes: the level of ownership of a foreign corporation required to designate it as a CFC; whether the foreign tax system is relevant to the operation of the CFC rules; the type of income or activities of the CFC subject to the rule; and the approach adopted in taxing the CFC.

7.2.1   The level of ownership of a foreign corporation required to designate it a CFC

CFC legislation applies when domestic shareholders have a "substantial influence" on the foreign corporation. However, each country has a different concept of "substantial influence". In most cases, "substantial influence" is defined as control, because of the assumption that only controlling shareholders can really influence the foreign company's distribution policy.

Generally speaking, most countries have one or two tests that must be met in order to qualify a foreign entity as a CFC: a single ownership test (each domestic shareholder must hold more than a certain percentage or interest of the foreign corporation), and a global domestic ownership test (domestic shareholders as a group must hold more than a certain percentage or interest of the foreign corporation). In this latter case, some countries consider every domestic shareholder in order to quantify the global domestic ownership percentage; others require a minimum ownership requirement test (in other words, each domestic shareholder must hold more than a certain percentage in order to be counted in the global percentage).

The tests can be structured in a formal or in a substantive way. As will be explained, formal tests are very simple (so that compliance and administrative costs stay low) but easy to manipulate. The more formal the tests are, and the higher the percentages of ownership, the easier it is for domestic shareholders to escape the application of CFC rules.

In order to avoid manipulation, some countries (as, for example, Australia, Italy, Israel and New Zealand) have more substantive tests (like *de facto* control tests) that make it harder for domestic shareholders to avoid CFC rules.

A subsidiary issue is the time of the year the ownership tests should be met: most countries check the status of the foreign company at the end of the year (this solution is very simple, but easy to manipulate); in other countries a foreign company may be considered a CFC at any time in the year (this solution is harder to manipulate, but quite complex to implement).

The US rule is very formal on this regard. Under Subpart F a foreign corporation is a CFC if any group of US shareholders, each holding an ownership stake of at least 10 percent, hold, by vote or value, over 50 percent of the foreign corporation. Being very formal, the US rules are relatively simple, but easy to manipulate. For example, if 11 US shareholders own as a group 100 percent of the stock of a foreign corporation, but each of them owns no more than 9.9 percent, the CFC legislation is not applicable. Likewise, if one US shareholder owns precisely 50 percent of a foreign corporation, and the rest of the stock is held by foreign investors, the CFC legislation is again not applicable.

7.2.2 The relevance of the foreign tax system to the operation of the CFC rules

In regard to this issue CFC rules can be divided into global and jurisdictional approaches.

Some countries (for example, the US, Canada, Indonesia, New Zealand, Israel and South Africa) apply their CFC rules to all CFCs wherever they are resident (or located) and regardless of the foreign tax rates. This first approach is defined as a global approach. In its pure version, domestic shareholders are taxed on only certain types of income (so-called "tainted income"). This is why this approach is also known as a transactional approach.

Other countries (for example, Japan, Italy, the UK, Germany, France, Australia, Denmark, Portugal, Spain, Sweden, Hungary, Argentina, Turkey and China) apply CFC rules only to foreign companies resident in low-tax jurisdictions. This second approach is defined as a jurisdictional (or entity) approach, because it focuses on the rules of the foreign tax jurisdictions. In its pure version, all types of income realized by CFCs are taxable. However, as we will see, many countries adopting the jurisdictional approach also focus on the types of income earned by the CFC.

The definitions of "low-tax jurisdictions" and "tainted income" are the two major points of comparison of CFC rules. Here, we will deal with the definition of "low-tax jurisdictions", while the next section will be dedicated to the definition of "tainted income".

Under the jurisdictional approach, there are many ways to define a low-tax jurisdiction. The basic guideline is that the territorial requirement has to be structured in both a substantial and simple way, in order to prevent the avoidance of the CFC rules or an unjustified complexity. The correct trade-off between substantiality and simplicity is thus fundamental in defining the territorial requirement of CFCs.

On the face of it, the global approach is much stricter than the jurisdictional approach because it does not identify target territories. It would seem that multinationals based in countries where a global approach has been adopted (like the US) could claim that they have difficulties in competing with those multinationals based in countries where a jurisdictional approach has been adopted (like Italy). This argument, however, is partially wrong.

In fact, the legislative details and mechanisms generally make the global and jurisdictional approaches very similar to each other. By analyzing the tax details and mechanisms of CFC rules, the result is that both global and jurisdictional approaches grant deferral or exemption with regard to high-tax income (which is typically active income because it is less mobile) while they avoid deferral or exemption with regard to low-tax income (which is typically movable passive income). First, CFC rules based on the transactional approach generally "kick out of the rules" coverage income earned in high-tax countries. For example, under Subpart F, if the tax rate of the country where the CFC is located is 90 percent or more of the US corporate tax rate, the CFC legislation is not applicable. Second, foreign tax credit is applicable to CFC income: the tax credit is equal to the taxes the CFC has to pay to local government. Even if the foreign tax credit has the main goal of avoiding international double taxation, it also makes the transactional approach very similar to the jurisdictional one: the CFC income is (partially) taxable in the hands of domestic shareholders only if the foreign jurisdiction has a lower effective tax rate than the domestic one (as is the case under the jurisdictional approach).

In conclusion, the distinction between the global and the jurisdictional approach is somewhat superficial: the tax mechanisms are different but the results are quite similar. A significant convergence between the two different approaches is thus observable in practice.

7.2.3 The type of income or activities of the CFC subject to the rule

Regarding the types of income and activities subject to the CFC rule, some countries adopt a tainted income approach (also known as the transactional approach), and other countries the total income approach (also known as the jurisdictional or entity approach).

Under the first approach (adopted, first, by the US in 1962), only the tainted income of the CFC is taxable to its shareholders.

Under the second approach (adopted, first, by Japan in 1978), either all or none of the foreign entity income is taxable. If the foreign entity is located in a low-tax jurisdiction, its income is fully taxable in the hands of domestic shareholders. If the foreign entity is not located in a low-tax jurisdiction, CFC rules are not applicable (in other words, foreign entity income is not taxable).

Under the transactional approach, the big issue is the definition of CFC income (in other words, tainted income). The most important category of tainted income common to most countries (namely, the US, Argentina, Australia, Canada, Denmark, Germany, Israel and New Zealand) is passive income (dividends, interest, royalties and capital gains). This is because passive income is very mobile and thus it is generally subject to lower tax rates, making tax deferral very attractive.

The other important category of passive income is base company income, which is active income with no real connection to the jurisdiction in which the CFC is located. Technically, this is defined as income from sale and services rendered between affiliated parties (located in different countries) when there is no significant modification of the product by the base company (US definition). In the US, this is one of the most controversial provisions of Subpart F, since US multinationals believe that this specific rule makes them less able to compete with other multinationals. For this reason, US taxpayers try to avoid this provision, by having CFCs buy goods from unrelated cost plus manufacturers and distributing them through unrelated commissionaires, with the CFC as "entrepreneur" retaining the bulk of the profit.

7.2.4   The approach adopted in taxing the CFC

Countries vary in how they tax CFCs. The US uses a deemed dividend approach, but most countries simply tax domestic shareholders (treating the CFC as a pass-through entity).

Countries generally do not directly tax CFCs because that might violate treaty obligations on taxing a foreign corporation that does not have a PE in the taxing country.

The piercing the veil approach is much simpler than the deemed dividend approach (especially when there is a chain of CFCs and the deemed dividends have to jump up the chain). Considering that customary international tax law has changed in the last decades, so that taxing the shareholders directly on CFC income is permissible, the US may consider changing its approach.

7.2.5   The problems of Subpart F

Subpart F used to be considered a tough CFC regime, but from 1994 to 2017 it was subject to numerous exceptions that have tended to render it much weaker than the CFC rules of other major countries. The most important of these are the active financing exception, which exempts most financial institutions for Subpart F, and the CFC to CFC look-through rule, which together with the regulatory check-the-box rules, makes Subpart F inapplicable to interest and royalty payments from high-tax to low-tax jurisdictions.

These exceptions enabled US-based multinationals to amass $3 trillion in low-tax jurisdictions offshore by 2017. This income was "trapped" in that it could not be brought back without paying tax on the dividends. Therefore, there was a lot of pressure on the US to enact a participation exemption like the ones adopted recently by Japan and the UK. In addition, the lack of a participation exemption before 2017 together with the high US corporate tax rate on US-source income has led numerous US companies to establish new parents in Ireland or the UK. This in turns enables them to pay interest and royalties from the old parent to the new one without triggering a deemed dividend, since the new parent is not a CFC even if it is majority owned by US public shareholders.

7.2.6   GILTI

In response to these problems, the US in 2017 enacted several measures to address the trapped income issue. First, it applied a one-time tax of 8 percent to non-liquid foreign assets and 15.5 percent to liquid foreign assets held by CFCs at the end of 2017, whether distributed or not. While lower than the full 35 percent tax rate that would have applied to the trapped income had it been distributed as a dividend, this transition resulted in a significant tax being imposed on the $3 trillion accumulated in CFCs, and in significant repatriations of such income. Second, the US adopted the participation exemption, so that future income of CFCs that is not Subpart F income can be repatriated without further tax (but with no indirect foreign tax credit for any foreign tax on the CFC).

On the face of it, these provisions converted the US from a "worldwide" to a "territorial" jurisdiction. However, in practice that is not the case because (a) US residents and citizens continue to be taxed on worldwide income, as are US corporations on income not earned through CFCs; (b) because of the GILTI rule, most US-based multinationals do not have much income eligible for the participation exemption.

GILTI is a new category of Subpart F income that imposes current tax at 10.5 percent (half the US domestic corporate rate of 21 percent) on income of CFCs that exceeds a 10 percent deemed return on their basis in tangible assets. Foreign tax credits are permitted to offset the GILTI tax up to 80 percent of the foreign tax, so that if the foreign tax is 13.125 percent, it eliminates the GILTI tax (80 percent of 13.125 percent = 10.5 percent). Averaging foreign taxes on GILTI among countries is permitted, but not foreign taxes on other types of foreign income.

Because most US-based multinationals do not have significant tangible assets in their CFCs, the effect of GILTI is to apply a minimum tax of 10.5 percent to all foreign source income of CFCs on a current basis. This means that with the adoption of GILTI, the US abolished deferral and became a true worldwide taxing jurisdiction, albeit with a lower rate for foreign source income earned through CFCs. This result is significantly different from the pre-2017 expectation that the US would adopt "territoriality" and exempt most income of CFCs from tax. The impact of GILTI could change over time, however, if US-based multinationals respond by shifting more tangible assets abroad.

7.2.7   FDII

The lower rate applicable to GILTI raised the concern that US-based multinationals will respond by shifting profits offshore (where the tax rate is 10.5 percent) from the US (where the tax rate is 21 percent). In response, the US also adopted the foreign derived intangible income (FDII) rule. Under FDII, a US corporation that earns income from exporting goods or services (including royalties) pays a lower 13.125 percent tax rate on such income, to the extent it exceeds a deemed 10 percent return on its basis in US tangible assets.

FDII was intended to encourage US multinationals that export goods or services to keep profits in the US, and to encourage foreign multinationals to shift profits into the US (FDII applies to goods and services that are imported and then re-exported, as well as to goods and services that are exported, modified, and then re-imported).

It remains to be seen whether FDII achieves its goals. So far, it has not attracted increased FDI, perhaps because foreign multinationals fear it may be changed, or because they can be subject to tax rates lower than 13.125 percent (US multinationals are already subject to a lower rate of 10.5 percent under GILTI). In addition, because FDII is contingent on export performance, it violates the WTO export subsidy rules, and may be challenged in that forum.

8 Outbound taxation: active income

Under the benefits principle active income is supposed to be taxed primarily at source. The residence jurisdiction then has the obligation to eliminate double taxation by granting either an exemption or a foreign tax credit.

Most large OECD jurisdictions and many developing countries grant a participation exemption for dividends from CFCs paid out of their active income. The US, Japan, and the UK are the most recent additions to this trend. The only exception is that sometimes the exemption is limited, for example, to 95 percent of the dividend to substitute for the denial of deductions allocable to the exempt income.

If an exemption system applies, the foreign tax credit becomes much less important, because it typically applies only to direct, in other words, withholding taxes, and those are tending to disappear as explained in Chapter 4. However, the problem with exemption systems is that they result in double non-taxation if the income is not taxed at source, and this leads to an increased incentive to shift income out of both high-tax source countries and high-tax residence countries into tax havens. Existing CFC rules are inadequate to stop this trend toward BEPS, as the OECD has recently recognized.

Thus, it is worth retaining the foreign tax credit, and if the OECD BEPS project results in added limits on exemptions, it may become more important again in the future. Ideally, all the G20 countries which are home to the vast majority of the world's multinationals, would currently tax their multinational enterprises (MNEs) on their foreign-source income with foreign tax credits. This will enable source countries to re-establish source-based taxation of active income without the pressure of tax competition. The US and the EU have taken significant steps in this direction by adopting the GILTI rules (US) and the Anti-Tax Avoidance Directive (EU). Because of this, the indirect credit is still important despite the spread of participation exemptions.

The remainder of this chapter will focus on the US foreign tax credit, because despite the adoption of the participation exemption and repeal of the regular indirect credit, GILTI carries with it indirect credits (albeit limited ones).

8.1   The three hoops

To obtain the foreign tax credit a US taxpayer needs to jump through three hoops. Failure to pass the first two results in no credit or deduction, while failure to pass the third results in a deduction (which is generally only worth $0.21 per $1 of foreign tax, as opposed to a dollar-for-dollar tax reduction under a credit).

8.1.1   Was a tax paid?

The first hoop requires the taxpayer to establish that a tax was paid. This requires proof, in the form of a receipt that a payment was made (which also establishes the date of payment for currency conversion purposes). Then it is necessary to establish that the payment was for a tax in the form of a general levy rather than a fee for services. Finally, the taxpayer must not receive either a refund of the amount paid or a subsidy that is based on the payment, and the tax cannot be conditioned on the availability of the foreign tax credit.

8.1.2   Who paid the tax?

This is an easier hoop to pass than first appears, because the question is not who bore the economic burden of the tax but rather on whom foreign law imposes the tax as a technical legal matter. Thus, even if a loan agreement makes it clear that the foreign borrower bears the burden of any withholding tax on the interest, the withholding tax is still creditable because foreign law treats it as a tax on the lender withheld by the borrower. This disjunction from economic reality has predictably led to tax shelters in the form of "foreign tax credit generators" in which the US taxpayer gets the foreign tax credit but does not bear the economic burden of the tax.

8.1.3   Was the tax creditable?

In order to be creditable a foreign tax must: (1) not be imposed on more than gross income; (2) allow for deductions similar to those allowed in the US; and (3) have a realization requirement. These are usually satisfied but there are quite a few disputed cases where the foreign tax may or may not be creditable.

8.2   The foreign tax credit limit

An unlimited foreign tax credit allows for a refund if the foreign tax rate is higher than the US rate. Not surprisingly this would lead the foreign country to raise its rate at the US Treasury's expense, so the US and other credit countries limit the foreign tax credit to the domestic tax rate times the amount of the taxpayer's foreign-source income. (This is the reason why taxpayers subject to US tax typically prefer to increase their foreign-source rather than US-source income.)

In addition, the US and other credit countries sometimes adopt further limits to segregate types of income, either per country or per category of income or both. The main US distinction is between active and passive income and cross-country averaging (to reduce overall foreign tax below the US tax rate) is possible. However, GILTI income and income from branches are treated as separate from other types of income.

8.3   The indirect credit

The US also grants an indirect credit for taxes imposed on the GILTI income of corporate taxpayers that own 10 percent by vote of a foreign corporation. When GILTI results in a deemed dividend, the percentage of foreign tax attributable to the distributed income is creditable, and the same rule applies to other deemed dividends under Subpart F.

However, in the case of GILTI income the credit is limited to 80 percent of the foreign tax rate. The combination of GILTI and the participation exemption means that a US parent with CFCs pays zero tax on any income of the CFCs that is not Subpart F income up to a deemed 10 percent return on tangible assets. Above that deemed return, the rate on GILTI is 10.5 percent, but since 80 percent of foreign taxes can be credited, the US parent will pay no US tax if it has foreign taxes at a rate of 13.125 percent (80 percent of 13.125 percent = 10.5 percent).

Cross-crediting among countries is permitted. These rules lead to an incentive to shift tangible assets abroad (to benefit from a zero rate) and to invest in countries with a tax rate higher than 10.5 percent (to benefit from cross-crediting). Overall, however, GILTI is expected to lead to higher taxes paid to the US on foreign source income, and potentially to a new wave of inversions.

9 The tax treaty network

There are currently over 3,000 bilateral income tax treaties in force around the world. Remarkably, about 80 percent of the text of any two tax treaties is identical because they all follow the OECD or UN model treaties, which themselves have become more similar to each other. It can therefore be argued that the treaties constitute an international tax regime that also constrains the domestic tax law choices of even the larger countries. No country can easily decide to abandon the ALS for transfer pricing or to tax foreign corporations that do not have a PE without violating all of its tax treaties.

Despite the traditional name for treaties ("Convention for the Avoidance of Double Taxation") the main purpose of tax treaties is not to prevent double taxation, which is generally prevented by unilateral exemption or credit, but to implement the benefits principle by shifting the tax on passive income from the source to the residence country, while allowing the source country to tax active income if it is attributable to a PE within it. This has led some to question whether developing countries gain from tax treaties since they typically lose revenue (because they are capital importing), but tax treaties are important to reassure both direct and portfolio investors that tax rates will remain bounded. There is empirical evidence that tax treaties increase foreign direct investment (FDI) into developing countries.

In addition, modern tax treaties (from 1981 onward) also put limits on double non-taxation, and the OECD BEPS project has further emphasized this role of treaties as equivalent to eliminating double taxation.

9.1 The definitional articles

Articles 1–5 of any tax treaty define its scope and terms. Article 1 typically restricts the treaty to residents of the two countries. This is achieved by including either in the treaty or in the commentary (which has persuasive or even binding legal force) a LOB provision designed to prevent tax treaty abuse by third-country residents. The history of LOB and the OECD BEPS project clarify that its goal is to prevent double non-taxation which might arise from allowing residents of tax havens to gain benefits under treaties which are in effect between non-haven countries.

Article 2 defines the taxes covered by the treaty, which are typically income taxes but not value added tax (VAT) (no treaty needed because of the destination principle) or social security and inheritance taxes, which are sometimes covered by separate treaties.

Article 3 provides general definitions and states that undefined terms are defined by the domestic law of the jurisdiction imposing the tax. Article 4 defines residence and attempts to prevent double residence by providing for tie breakers. Article 5 defines PE in the way discussed in Chapter 5.

9.2   The substantive articles

Article 6 provides that income from real property can be taxed fully at source, and the same usually applies to capital gains from real property. Article 7 permits source-based taxation of active income if attributable to a PE. Article 8 provides for pure residence taxation of shipping and air traffic. Article 9 sets forth the ALS for transfer pricing, which is implemented by the OECD Transfer Pricing Guidelines.

The core of the treaty is Articles 10–13, which shift taxation of passive income from the source to the residence countries by reducing withholding taxes. The withholding tax on dividends is typically 5 percent for direct dividends and 15 percent for portfolio dividends. The withholding tax on interest, royalties and capital gains is typically zero. "Other income" (including, for example, income from derivatives) is likewise not subject to tax at source under the OECD model (but not the UN model, which also permits higher withholding tax rates in Articles 10–13).

Finally, Article 23A provides for exemption and Article 23B for credit to prevent double taxation.

9.3   The procedural articles

Article 24 provides for non-discrimination for nationals as well as residents. Article 25 is the dispute resolution mechanism and traditionally it provided only for negotiations between the "competent authorities" of each country, although recently binding arbitration has become more common and it is included in the OECD model.

9.4   Exchange of information

Recently, a lot of emphasis has been put on exchange of information as a way of preventing tax avoidance by residents. Traditional limits on government access to information, like bank secrecy laws, have been lifted and most tax havens have entered into Tax Information Exchange Agreements. The OECD has recently put forth a Multilateral Agreement for Administrative Assistance in Tax Matters, which calls for automatic exchange of information and has been signed by over 80 countries. It remains to be seen, however, whether this effort will significantly curb tax evasion, which remains rampant in many countries around the world.

9.5   The multilateral instrument

As part of the BEPS project, the OECD has drafted a multilateral instrument (MLI) that modifies the tax treaties to prevent double non-taxation. Over 80 countries have signed the MLI (not including the US) and over 10 have ratified it.

When two countries that have a bilateral tax treaty both ratify the MLI, its provisions modify the tax treaty between them. However, with the exception of a few "minimum standards", most provisions of the MLI are elective and each pair of countries can choose which ones to implement. The most important minimum standard is the requirement to include in the treaty either an LOB provision or a primary purpose test stating that the treaty should be interpreted to prevent transactions if one of their primary purposes was to achieve double non-taxation.

PART II

Selected Contemporary Issues

10 Three steps forward, one step back? Reflections on "Google taxes" and the destination-based corporate tax

10.1   Introduction: why is the corporate tax robust?

A large puzzle underlies the recent G20 and OECD BEPS project. If the scope of BEPS is as broad as the reports suggest, why are corporate tax revenues in the OECD so robust?

The final OECD report on BEPS Action 11 suggests that BEPS activities result in between $100 and $240 billion in annual lost revenue from corporate income tax (CIT) on a global basis. The wide spread between these two numbers indicates the significant uncertainty involved. In addition, the higher number represents a relatively small portion of total global CIT revenues, since it is only about half of the annual CIT revenue of the US alone. Moreover, overall OECD revenue data do not indicate that BEPS has had a significant impact on CIT revenue, since those have held steady at 8–10 percent of total revenue since the 1980s (i.e., before BEPS became a significant issue).

These data are surprising in light of what we know about the extent of tax avoidance by US multinationals. Currently, US-based multinationals have accumulated over $2.5 trillion in low-tax jurisdictions offshore, and the US tax on that income (most of which has been accumulated since 2005, when a one-year amnesty allowed previous profits to be repatriated) is about $800 billion, which is also the ten-year estimate of the cost of deferral to the US Treasury. These data suggest that if the OECD estimate is right, a very high percentage of total BEPS activity is due to US multinationals.

This estimate suggests that US tax policy is important to the rest of the world, including Europe and the Nordic region. The US is the largest economy in the world. If the US were to tax its multinationals more effectively, this would make it much easier for smaller economies to do the same without worrying about competition from low-taxed US multinationals.

How do other countries avoid large-scale BEPS activities by their own multinationals? One explanation is that most of them have more robust CFC rules than the US. Since the enactment of check the box (1997) and the CFC-to-CFC payments rule (2006), the US CFC rules (Subpart F) have essentially become toothless, except in preventing repatriations. Other OECD countries tend to have more robust CFC rules which explicitly impose taxes on income accumulated in low-tax jurisdictions and having no real connection to that jurisdiction. If the US had CFC rules like Germany, France or Japan, the extent of low-taxed income of US multinationals would be significantly reduced.

Another explanation for the relative robustness of the CIT base to BEPS is the gradual downward ratcheting of the PE threshold. The PE threshold is entrenched in all the tax treaties and prevents source jurisdictions from taxing business profits of non-resident enterprises unless they have a PE in the source jurisdiction, which in turn requires some kind of physical presence directly or through an agent. This rule is clearly obsolete in the twenty-first century, but it is hard to change given its importance in the treaties. But over the past decade there has been a trend to gradually reduce the threshold, for example, by treating subsidiaries as the agents of their parent corporations and thus treating the parent as having a PE through its subsidiary. In addition, the invention of the "service PE" makes it easier to subject service providers to tax without much physical presence. A 2012 decision by the Spanish Economic Administrative Court went even further and held that an Irish company making sales through a website that was hosted outside Spain but that focused on the Spanish market, had a "virtual PE" in Spain.

Since the market is less subject to tax competition pressures than the location of headquarters or production facilities, reducing the PE threshold makes it easier to prevent BEPS. This has recently led some jurisdictions to enact new taxes aimed specifically at structures that seek to exploit the domestic market while avoiding a PE. This chapter will discuss these taxes in the UK, Australia, and India, explore their relationship to the BEPS project, and then consider whether further steps can be taken toward a destination-based corporate tax (DBCT) that will be a permanent cure for BEPS.

10.2   The three "Google taxes"

10.2.1   The UK's "diverted profits tax"

Even before BEPS was concluded, the UK enacted the "diverted prof-its tax" (DPT) that became effective on April 1, 2015. The DPT is intended primarily to address structures like Google's Double Irish Dutch Sandwich, which is contained in the guidance published by HMRC as Example 3.

Under Example 3, the US parent of a multinational group (Company A) owns a subsidiary incorporated in Ireland that is treated under Irish law as resident in a tax haven (Company D) which owns the IP for the rest of the world. Company D licenses the IP to Company C in the Netherlands, which in turn licenses it to Company B in Ireland. Company B owns Company E which provides sales and service support in the UK, with all sales contracts being finalized by Company B in Ireland.

Under this structure, UK tax is only applied to the cost plus profits of Company E, which are minimal. Companies B, C, and D do not have a PE in the UK and are not subject to tax. Company B is taxable in Ireland, but most of its profits are payable as a royalty to Company C, which in turn pays most of its profits to Company D in the tax haven. There is no withholding tax on the payment from Company B to C (because of the Ireland–Netherlands tax treaty) or from C to D (because the Netherlands does not tax outbound royalties). The US CFC rules do not apply because other than Company D, all the other entities in the group are disregarded under check the box, and their activities attributed to Company D (regarded under the US rules as resident in Ireland).

The DPT subjects this arrangement to UK tax because Company B's affairs are arranged so as to avoid a UK PE. The section 86 charge will apply where: there is a non-UK resident company (Company B) that is carrying on a trade; a UK resident (Company E, the "avoided PE") that is carrying on activities in the UK in connection with the supply of goods or services by Company B; it is reasonable to assume that the activity of Company E or Company B was designed to avoid Company B being subject to UK CIT; there is a "tax mismatch" in that the tax paid by Company B in Ireland is less than 80 percent of the tax avoided by Company E ; and tax reduction was one of the main purposes of the arrangement.

If these conditions are satisfied, a 25 percent DPT applies to the diverted profits (i.e., the profits that would have been taxable to Company B in the UK if it had had a PE), measured initially as 30 percent of the deductions taken by Company B, with later adjustments (and credits for any foreign tax).

The DPT has been criticized for contradicting the UK tax treaties in substance, which require an actual PE. HMRC has defended it as a new tax that is not subject to the treaties, and this issue is unlikely to arise because UK treaties are not "self executing" and have not been applied to the DPT by legislation. This means that a UK taxpayer cannot challenge the DPT as inconsistent with a UK tax treaty.

10.2.2   The Australian anti-avoidance tax

In May 2015, the Australian government released the tax integrity Multinational Anti-Tax Avoidance Law (MAAL), which was designed to "prevent foreign corporations from using complex, contrived and artificial schemes that enable them to have substantial sales activities in Australia, but pay little or no tax anywhere". Unlike the DPT, this is not a new tax, but an amendment to Australia's general anti-abuse rule (GAAR) (Part IVA of the Income Tax Assessment Act (ITAA) 1936). The MAAL became effective on January 1, 2016 for enterprises with annual income over AUD 1 billion.

New ITAA section 177DA applies if a non-resident of Australia sells goods or services to an unrelated Australian resident, income from such sales is not attributable to a PE, and activities are undertaken by an Australian associate of the provider in connection with the sale. Under these circumstances, if it is reasonable to conclude that the scheme is designed to avoid income attributable to a PE and tax reduction was a principal purpose, the ATO is free to disregard the arrangement.

This rule was likewise designed to address structures like the "Double Irish Dutch Sandwich". The Explanatory Materials contain an example of B Company that provides supplies in Australia and owns SubCo in Australia to provide support; all contracts are entered into with B Company which pays a large royalty to C Company, located in a non-tax jurisdiction, with no withholding tax. Under those circumstances, B Company would be treated as having a PE in Australia, and the royalty from B to C Company treated as an expense incurred by the PE and subject to withholding tax.

The MAAL has been defended as consistent with Australia's tax treaties because it is an anti-avoidance rule, and the PE limit should not apply when the business profits are not taxed by the country of residence. In addition, treaty overrides are possible in Australia, so a treaty-based challenge to the MAAL is unlikely.

10.2.3   The Indian equalization tax

In February 2016, Indian Finance Minister Shri Arun Jaitley proposed as part of Finance Bill 2016 an "equalization levy" on certain digital transactions into India. This proposal followed a loss by the Indian revenue authorities in the Right Florists case, where the Income Tax Appellate Tribunal rules that payments by residents to Google and Yahoo for advertising services aimed at the Indian market could not be taxed because they were business profits and the providers did not have a PE in India.

The equalization levy is a 6 percent withholding tax applied to the gross consideration paid by Indian service recipients engaged in a business to a non-resident that does not have a PE in India for online advertisement and related services, if the total amount exceeds INR 100,000.

The equalization levy has been criticized as inconsistent with India's tax treaties. However, since it is a new tax that is explicitly not imposed on net income, it is hard to see how the treaties apply.

10.3   BEPS

The original BEPS action plan explicitly stated that there would not be a fundamental change to the PE rule. While Action 7 addresses some situations of avoided PEs, the fundamental PE rules including physical presence remain unchanged.

Action 1 was supposed to address the challenges of the digital economy and in particular consider revising the PE concept. However, in the end the Final Report only mentions three options (a nexus-based approach based on significant economic presence, a withholding tax on digital transactions, and an equalization levy) without recommending any. However, the report leaves the door open to countries that wish to adopt such measures "subject to their treaty obligations".

While option 1 (replacing the PE threshold with significant economic presence) and 2 (a new withholding tax on sale proceeds in lieu of income tax) seem to require modifying the treaties, option 3 (equalization tax) does not seem to require treaty modification since it is a new tax. This is presumably why India adopted it, while Australia chose to adopt a new anti-avoidance regime that is arguably consistent with its treaties (under the OECD view, anti-abuse measures are generally not seen as inconsistent with treaties). The UK presumably acted before the scope of BEPS was known.

Overall, while the failure of BEPS to address the shortcomings of the PE standard can be seen as a step backward to the nineteenth century (when the concept was invented), there is enough flexibility for countries to act unilaterally and still be treaty-compliant.

10.4   Toward destination-based corporate tax?

Overall, however, these steps are insufficient to address the broad scope of the BEPS phenomenon. They point in the right direction – a corporate tax based on the location of the customers, who are less mobile than the multinationals. But they are tied to an existing PE standard, since both the UK and the Australian proposals require a presence in the country to apply. The equalization tax is not so limited, but since it is a gross-based tax the rate is quite low.

The alternative, as various scholars have suggested, is a DBCT. Under DBCT, MNEs would be treated as unitary businesses and taxed based on where they sell their goods or services, i.e., on a destination basis rather than (as in current corporate taxes) primarily on an origin basis.

In recent years, DBCT has attracted some support from economists, such as Alan Auerbach and Mike Devereux. While the economists tend to advocate a cash flow DBCT, i.e., a corporate tax that is more consumption- than income-based because MNEs would be allowed to expense capital outlays, both types of taxes apply to corporate rents in the same way. Moreover, the economists' proposals raise similar issues to older DBCT proposals, e.g., in regard to compatibility with treaties or with WTO rules. One important difference between the Auerbach/Devereux proposal and earlier ones is that under Auerbach/Devereux, the tax is imposed on the full value of imports, like a VAT, with no deduction for cost of goods sold. This feature plus expensing make the DBCT more a consumption tax than a destination-based CIT.

These proposals have attracted significant critiques, e.g., from Rosanne Altshuler, Harry Grubert, and Susan Morse. I would like to use this opportunity to restate the case for DBCT and reply to some of the common objections to it.

10.4.1 Three reasons for DBCT

There are three major reasons to adopt DBCT. The first two apply to all unitary tax (UT) proposals: corporate residence is relatively meaningless so that a method is needed to tax MNEs at source; and the distinction between subsidiaries and branches is artificial and should be discarded. The third supports DBCT specifically, in that it addresses tax competition in a way that other UT proposals do not.

Corporate residence is meaningless

As Dan Shaviro has emphasized, corporate residence is a not very meaningful concept because (a) corporations are not physically present anywhere, (b) corporations are not meaningfully subject to redistribution because the incidence of the corporate tax is not on them, (c) corporations do not vote, and (d) even the location of corporate headquarters, which is a more meaningful concept than place of incorporation, can be moved. The last point is particularly important in the age of inversions. While the first wave of inversions could be effectively combated by adopting a managed and controlled definition of corporate residency because the top management would not move to Bermuda, this is less effective now that the UK is an attractive location for headquarters. Thus, it would be preferable to have a way of taxing MNEs that does not depend on the residence of the corporate parent and does not draw an increasingly artificial distinction between US- and foreign-based MNEs, such as UT.

Subsidiaries are branches

In the age of check the box, the distinction between subsidiaries and branches is meaningless. Most MNEs are directed from one central location as a unitary business, and it does not make sense to tax them based on treating subsidiaries but not branches as separate taxpayers. This undermines the arm's length principle and leads directly to UT.

Tax competition

Once the necessity of UT is accepted, the argument for DBCT is that the consumer base is less subject to tax competition than the location either of property or of payroll. The property factor is in any case problematic because of the need for valuation and because the most important type of property of a modern MNE is IP, which is just as evanescent as the MNE itself. As for payroll, from a unilateral US perspective it makes no sense to adopt a rule that would encourage shifting more jobs overseas.

10.4.2   Objections

Below are my replies to some common objections to DBCT, as summarized for example by Altshuler, Grubert, and Morse.

Why not a VAT?

One common reaction to DBCT proposals is that it makes no sense to have an income tax based on the location of consumption, whereas a consumption tax like the VAT should be destination-based. Admittedly, the DBCT is not a consumption tax (even the Auerbach/ Devereux cash flow DBCT allows a deduction for wages, so it is not entirely equivalent to a VAT) but in a unilateral context there are good reasons for it, as explained below. The fact that the tax base to be apportioned based on sales is a net base and not a gross base (wages are deductible and capital expenditures are not in my version) means that it is still a corporate income tax and not a consumption tax. As discussed below, it makes more sense to have a balanced formula in a multilateral setting, but a destination-based formula is more likely to win acceptance from the many countries that import more than they export.

Tax planning

Another common objection is that it is very easy to tax plan around a DBCT by having the MNE sell goods or services to an independent distributor in a tax haven that will then resell at a low profit margin into the US. But most MNEs would be reluctant to give up control over distribution, and if they do not, the distributor is not independent and can be looked through. Moreover, even with a truly independent distributor, look-through can be applied if there is no meaningful change in the goods or services being provided. Similar rules already apply under the base company rule in Subpart F, and both the Avi-Yonah, Clausing, and Durst legislative language and the Market Fairness Act include language designed to address this issue. The ultimate destination is determined in most VAT contexts and can also be determined in a DBCT.

Treaties/PE

A third objection is that DBCT violates the tax treaties because it will tax MNEs who sell into the US without a PE. But it is not easy to avoid having a PE, or else e-commerce would have already eliminated source-based corporate tax for sellers into the US. And if there is a PE, the residual force of attraction rule can be used to attribute all sales income to the PE. In addition, the OECD is rethinking the PE concept and various countries have modified it, so that it may be time to substitute a numerical threshold for the current PE, even if this requires a treaty override.

WTO

Another objection is that DBCT violates the WTO rules for export subsidies since direct taxes cannot be border-adjusted. The distinction between direct and indirect taxes under WTO rules is not entirely clear; consumption tax proposals in the US typically argue that they do not violate the rule even if they are not VATs because of the deduction for wages. Nor is it clear why DBCT is objectionable if it applies to all US sales by both domestic and foreign sellers, similarly to a VAT. But assuming DBCT is a WTO violation, it will take many years of litigation to reach the sanctions stage, during which the US can renegotiate the WTO rules or persuade other countries to accept DBCT. No WTO challenge has been launched against US state DBCTs despite calls to do so, and this issue is ultimately a political question.

Tax equity

It has also been argued that DBCT discriminates against developing countries that export more than they import and will therefore lose revenue. This is not true overall, since the BRICS would benefit from DBCT as they are immense markets, and other developing countries are already impacted by tax competition. In other cases adjustments can be made, but this is hardly an argument against unilateral US adoption of DBCT. If the US were to adopt DBCT, this would put pressure on other countries to do the same, since otherwise multinationals that export could move to the US and pay non-tax on exports to other countries. Eventually, this is likely to lead either to agreement on a balanced formula (like the EU's Common Consolidated Corporate Tax Base proposal) or to worldwide adoption of DBCT.

Double taxation

Perhaps the most important debate is about how other countries would adjust to the US adopting DBCT. Avi-Yonah, Clausing, and Durst have argued that there would be a lot of pressure on other countries to follow suit because otherwise their MNEs would move to the US and export from there. Morse argues that this is not true because they can abolish their corporate tax or at least grant tax holidays. But in that case there would be no double taxation, and the most cogent argument against DBCT is the concern that both origin and destination countries will tax the same income. In my opinion it is always better to put the onus of preventing such double taxation on the MNEs themselves; if they do not like it, let them move to the US or lobby the origin country for a tax holiday (which they do anyway, but under current rules that result in double non-taxation of immense amounts of income). If there is to be a single tax on MNEs, from a US perspective it is better that it be a DBCT one than an origin-based one.

10.5   Conclusion

The UK, Australian, and Indian attempts to impose tax on foreign corporations deriving extensive revenue from the domestic market without a PE all indicate that in the presence of BEPS, taxation based on the market is a way to ensure the continued robustness of the CIT. While the OECD retreated from its initial commitment to addressing the digital economy, it has left sufficient leeway for countries to move forward unilaterally. If the US, for example, were to adopt DBCT, it is likely that other countries would follow, like they did when the US adopted CFC rules. This may well be the twenty-first century way to protect the CIT base against BEPS.

11 Evaluating BEPS

11.1 Introduction: the financial crisis and inequality

The financial crisis of 2008 and the Great Recession that followed have raised anew the problem of how to address a growing inequality both between the rich and everybody else within countries, and between developed and developing countries. Both dimensions of inequality, the intra- and inter-country ones, have risen in this century, and the Great Recession has made both problems worse. The current rise of populism in both the US and in Europe, and the vehement reactions to a tide of migrants from poorer to richer countries, show how these two problems are intertwined.

Sixteen years ago, I wrote about the challenge that globalization and tax competition pose to the fiscal viability of the post-World War II welfare state. I pointed out that if tax evasion by rich individuals and tax avoidance by multinational corporations is allowed to undermine the ability of both developed and developing countries to provide adequate social insurance for their citizens, a violent reaction against globalization may ensue that risks ending this era of opening borders, just like World War I ended the previous era of globalization a century ago. In 2018, I worry that the lack of adequate response to the Great Recession is leading to the rise of violent anti-globalization sentiments on both the right and the left, embodied in the US by the success of Bernie Sanders and Donald Trump, and in Europe by an even more virulent rejection of the open border policies for which the EU stands.

It is imperative for the West to find ways to strengthen the ability of the state to provide adequate social insurance and to reduce inequality, before these forces lead to the closing of the borders and to pressures that could result in the end of the current era of globalization. But the response so far has unfortunately not been adequate.

Following the financial crisis and ensuing austerity, politicians discovered the problem of tax avoidance. On the corporate tax avoidance front, the OECD and G20 launched the BEPS project in 2013, and in October 2015 this culminated with the release of a series of action steps that the OECD and G20 countries undertook to adopt. OECD Secretary-General Angel Gurria stated that

> Base erosion and profit shifting affects all countries, not only economically, but also as a matter of trust. BEPS is depriving countries of precious resources to jump-start growth, tackle the effects of the global economic crisis and create more and better opportunities for all. But beyond this, BEPS has been also eroding the trust of citizens in the fairness of tax systems worldwide. The measures we are presenting today represent the most fundamental changes to international tax rules in almost a century: they will put an end to double non-taxation, facilitate a better alignment of taxation with economic activity and value creation, and when fully implemented, these measures will render BEPS-inspired tax planning structures ineffective.[1]

Is Gurria justified in his optimism? I do not think so. These efforts are commendable and to some extent have an impact. But in my opinion they are inadequate. The basic problem is that they take as a given the fundamental consensus underlying the international tax regime (ITR), also known as the "benefits principle". Under the benefits principle, active (business) income should be taxed primarily at source while passive (investment) income should be taxed primarily at residence. This compromise between the claims of residence and source countries was reached in 1923 and still serves as the foundation of ITR. It is embedded in over 3,000 bilateral tax treaties and in the domestic laws of the US and most other countries. Not surprisingly, it is also reflected in BEPS, which is an attempt to improve source-based taxation of active income.

In my opinion, the benefits principle should be reconsidered, because the reliance on source-based taxation for active income and residence based taxation for active income requires cooperation by too many jurisdictions. The problems of BEPS stem from its reliance on the benefits principle.

---

1 OECD, Centre for Tax Policy and Administration, *OECD presents outputs of OECD/G20 BEPS Project for discussion at G20 Finance Ministers meeting*, October 5, 2015.

In the case of active income, the justification for taxation at source has been that most of such income is earned by corporations that have no fixed residence. However, since the 1980s, tax competition has led many source jurisdictions to offer tax holidays to multinationals, and residence jurisdictions are reluctant to tax their multinational on their global income so as not to put them at a competitive disadvantage. The result has been that most multinationals are not taxed currently at source or at residence.

Two recent examples can be used to illustrate the problem of tax avoidance on cross-border income:

As of the end of 2015, US multinationals had over $2 trillion in offshore profits in low-taxed jurisdictions. This amount, which translates to about $700 billion in US taxes avoided, is mostly income that was economically earned in the US and shifted offshore to jurisdictions like Singapore, Ireland, or Luxembourg, which have effective tax rates in single digits.

How do the multinationals do it? A couple of examples can suffice. Apple, Inc. is the world's largest company by market capitalization. Most of its billions in profits relate to intellectual property developed at its headquarters in Cupertino, California. But for tax purposes, most of the profit is booked in its Irish subsidiaries – let's call them Apple Ireland.

Some of the profit shifting is achieved through a "cost sharing agreement" (CSA). Cost sharing is a concept developed in IRS regulations in the 1980s, but which became more significant due to the increasing importance of IP. The idea behind cost sharing is this: when a US multinational begins a new research project (for example, a search for a drug to treat a certain disease), it can agree to share the costs of development with its offshore subsidiaries. Then, if the project is successful, the parties share the profits in the same proportions. For example, if Apple Ireland contributed 80 percent of the costs of developing the iPhone 6, it would get 80 percent of the profit. Importantly, none of the actual work is done by Apple Ireland. Apple just gives Apple Ireland the money and Apple Ireland pays it back as its contribution to the research costs.

Why would the IRS regulations permit this? Because if the research failed, then the taxpayer would lose its ability to deduct the costs sent offshore. The more of the cost sent offshore, the more deductions would be at risk. So the IRS thought there was a natural limit to tax-payer willingness to share costs with offshore affiliates.

That analysis may have been true for Big Pharma, which usually waits to enter into a CSA with an offshore affiliate until a drug has passed its initial trials and is well on its way to a patent, and then battles the IRS over valuation issues at the time the CSA was executed. But the same analysis makes no sense for Apple, since if there is anything certain in business, it is that a new version of the iPhone will sell.

There is another trick involved in Apple Ireland's profitability. Another portion of its profits derives from countries where Apple sells the iPhones. Apple Ireland licenses the right to use Apple's brand and IP to Apple affiliates in other countries. Those affiliates in turn pay Apple Ireland hefty royalties, which operate to shift the sales profits gained in those countries to Ireland.

Before 1997, such a scheme would not have worked, because the royal-ties received by Apple Ireland would have triggered a tax in the US under so-called Subpart F. But in 1997 the Clinton Administration adopted the "check the box" rule. Under this rule, Apple Ireland can treat all of its foreign affiliates as if they did not exist as separate entities for US tax purposes, and treat the money they paid to Apple Ireland as income earned in Ireland. The result is that for US tax purposes there are no royalties and no US tax triggered by them, because Apple Ireland treats the money as its own sales income.

The Obama Administration promised to repeal check the box; this was the biggest international revenue-raiser in the first Obama budget. But by November 2009 the Administration recanted under pressure from the multinationals. Eventually, President Obama signed into law a five-year extension of a provision (first enacted by a Republican Congress as a "temporary" measure in 2006) that enshrined check the box in the tax law.

Finally, the Senate hearing revealed two Irish-specific tricks used by Apple. Ireland has a tax rate of 12.5 percent, far below the US rate of 35 percent. But Apple did not want to pay even 12.5 percent. Its solution was ingenious: for US tax purposes, Apple Ireland is treated as an Irish company because it is incorporated in Ireland, so it is not taxed by the US. But for Irish tax purposes, Apple Ireland was treated as an American company because it is "managed and controlled" from California. As a result, Apple Ireland claimed it was a tax resident nowhere. On top of that, it negotiated a sweetheart tax deal with Ireland for its Irish income that resulted in its paying a tax rate of less than 2 percent.

These types of tricks are used by most US multinationals. If the primary driver of value of a US multinational is IP developed in the US, the Apple scheme can simply be replicated.

But what if the value derives from more traditional, tangible items? Some US multinationals do pay higher taxes (e.g., the car companies). But others try to avoid tax nevertheless. Caterpillar, Inc. is a good example.

Caterpillar does not make a lot of money on the heavy equipment it manufactures. But it does make money on replacement parts, because once you buy a Caterpillar bulldozer, you will need parts, which you can obtain only from Caterpillar at a huge mark-up. Caterpillar prides itself on its ability to deliver parts within 24 hours anywhere in the world, including the Arctic tundra (where its equipment is used in mineral extraction).

Before 1998, Caterpillar bought the parts from unrelated manufacturers and stored them at its warehouse in Morton, Illinois. When a dealer requested a part for a customer overseas, Caterpillar "sold" (but did not actually ship) the part to a Swiss subsidiary which in turn sold the part to the unrelated dealer.

The problem, according to accounting firm PriceWaterhouseCoopers (PwC), was that Caterpillar's sale of the part to its Swiss subsidiary triggered US tax. Much better, PwC said, would be if the parts were sold by the manufacturer directly to the Swiss subsidiary which could then sell it to the dealer.

Fine, said Caterpillar, but we do not want to change our operations. So in exchange for $60 million in fees, PwC came up with a way to lower Caterpillar's US tax without changing its operations. PwC's solution was for the manufacturers to bill the Swiss subsidiary for the parts but continue to ship them to the Illinois warehouse which continued to transport them to Caterpillar's foreign customers. If the parts were shipped overseas, they were deemed to have been "owned" by the Swiss subsidiary, and PwC devised a virtual inventory to track them even though the parts were indistinguishably commingled in the warehouse. The result was that Caterpillar continued to run its parts business from the US, but declared 85 percent or more of the parts profits in Switzerland.

The IRS has now challenged this billing arrangement, which resulted in shifting some $2.4 billion in Caterpillar profits from the United States to Switzerland. A Grand Jury has issued subpoenas under a criminal investigation for tax fraud.

But the disturbing fact is that the whole story would not have come to light but for a whistleblower, who alerted both the US Senate Permanent Subcommittee on Investigations and the IRS. And while Caterpillar is facing a court challenge, in most cases of corporate tax avoidance, like Apple, the IRS's hands are tied because what Apple did may have been legal under the US tax code.

The fundamental problem of BEPS stems from its reliance on the benefits principle. BEPS seeks to bolster source-based taxation of active income, but it does not apply to countries outside the OECD/G20, and its scope is quite limited as discussed below.

To preserve income tax in the twenty-first century, multilateral solutions are needed. BEPS is multilateral, but it is hampered by the fact that there are too many source jurisdictions for active income. If we reversed the benefits principle so that passive income is taxed primarily at source and active income at residence, far fewer jurisdictions will need to cooperate.

For passive income, the number of source jurisdictions is much smaller than residence jurisdictions. Because most individuals are relatively risk averse, portfolio investment flows overwhelmingly to a small number of countries – the US, the EU, and Japan. Even the BRICs countries (Brazil, Russia, India, China) mostly attract portfolio investment through mutual funds that are relatively easy to tax. Thus, if the "big three" can coordinate to reinstate a withholding tax on interest, dividends, and royalties flowing from them, most of the problem of taxing passive income can be solved. Crucially, money cannot stay in tax havens and earn decent rates of return, so the cooperation of tax havens is not needed.

For active income, about 90 percent of large multinationals are head-quartered in the G20, and none of those countries have a tax rate below 20 percent. Therefore, if multinationals were taxed on a coordinated basis and had restricted ability to move out, most of the problem would be resolved.

I would therefore suggest that we reconsider the benefits principle in light of the reality of globalization. We should tax passive income primarily at source and active income primarily at residence.

Importantly, as with current rules, this does not preclude the alternative. Once passive income is taxed at source, taxpayers may be able to credit the tax upon declaring it to their residence country. And once active income is taxed at residence, a credit can be given to source country taxes if the source country responds to the limitation of tax competition by reimposing its tax. But the key is that the income has already been taxed, so that no double non-taxation ensues even if taxpayers do not declare the income (in the case of passive income, where the residence rate may be higher) or source countries choose not to tax in the case of active income.

The following unpacks this analysis in more detail. Section 11.2 analyzes the BEPS response to corporate tax avoidance and its shortcomings. Section 11.3 develops the alternative: taxing passive income primarily at source and active income primarily at residence. The chapter concludes in Section 11.4.

11.2   The limits of the BEPS project

On October 5, 2015, the OECD and G20 released the final BEPS package of 13 reports, which cover 15 actions. It was only two years since the G20 leaders had endorsed the ambitious and comprehensive Action Plan to address BEPS at the meeting in St Petersburg on September 5–6, 2013.

The BEPS package represents the first substantial – and overdue – renovation of the international tax standards in almost a century. It is an unprecedented turning point in the history of international tax law. The mission of the BEPS package is to align the location of taxable profits with the location of economic activities and value creation. Some generally accepted principles of international tax law, including the single tax principle, the benefit principle, the anti-discrimination principle, and the transparency principle have been reflected in many respects.

Despite considerable progress, there are many shortcomings with the BEPS project due to the short two-year framework. Hence, the BEPS project is not the final destination of international tax law reform. In fact, it is the first step toward the modernization of global tax governance in the long run.

11.2.1   New shoes on the old road: an old approach for the new destination

The primary problem with the BEPS project is that although the new destination has been redefined, new principles and new rules have not been truly established for the new direction, and the old principles have been strengthened by a patch-up of current rules.

The core principle of international tax law is the single tax principle, which requires eradication of both double taxation and double non-taxation. Unfortunately, both the governments and the MNES have been active in fighting against the double taxation, and have ignored another danger of double non-taxation. Therefore, the main theme of traditional international tax law has been eradication of double taxation, instead of double non-taxation.

Based on the single tax principle, the mission of the BEPS project is to prevent and eliminate the double non-taxation. As the G20 leaders pointed out, "profits should be taxed where economic activities deriving the profits are performed and where value is created".[2] Therefore, the new direction of international tax law reform in the context of BEPS project is to safeguard the single tax principle by fighting against the BEPS.

It is well known that the rickety ITR, including rules and underlying principles, is one of the primary root causes of BEPS opportunities. Therefore, the new direction demands revolutionary changes to current approaches. The ideal roadmap for the BEPS project is supposed to replace the old principles with a new principle, and to redesign the rules based on the requirement of the new principle.

---

2   Tax Annex to the St Petersburg Declaration, September 2013.

Unfortunately, many old principles of international tax law have been preserved and continued in the final BEPS package. The mixture of new and old principles has substantially compromised the value of the new principle, and made the legal reform of international tax look more like the patch-up of existing rules and principles. The reason is pretty obvious. On the one hand, it is impossible to abolish or even reconsider the dysfunctional current rules, which have been favored by some large countries and MNEs. On the other hand, it is mandatory to change the current rules to some extent, because of the emerging political pressure against BEPS schemes.

Given the fact that two years are very short for serious in-depth research, debate, and negotiation, given the strong tradition and interest groups' desire to keep the continuity of old principles, given the global voice for closing up the BEPS opportunities, the architect of the BEPS project has no choice but to patch up some loopholes of current rules, instead of fundamental restructuring the current regime.

As a result, complete renovation of current international tax law did not happen, and genuine new rules guided by the new principle have not been formulated. Moreover, the patch-up work has produced many more complex, discretionary, uncertain, costly, and, in many cases, contradictory rules. There are two possible negative consequences. First, it is difficult to translate all the new rules into the reality. Second, even if the BEPS project is implemented as outlined and promised, it is still possible for the creation of either new BEPS opportunities on the part of MNEs, or arbitrariness on the part of tax authorities.

In addition to adhering to the independent entity principle and rejection of the new principle of single unitary entity, the BEPS project is also silent on the basic concepts of residence and source, and where profit should be considered to be earned. As the existing rules based on the old principles have been strengthened, and new rules based on the new principle have not been established, the BEPS project is not so revolutionary and fundamental as it appeared at first sight.

The ironic fact is that the patch-up of current rules in the BEPS project was made in the name of new mission and new principle. However, because of the inconsistencies and conflicts between the new principle and old principles, the new principle of international tax law has been compromised or undermined by the strengthened current rules based on old principles. Without the support of new principle and new rules, it is very challenging to achieve the new destination of aligning the taxation of MNE profits with economic activity.

11.2.2   The survival and continuity of notional and illusionary independent entity principle and arm's length principle

The traditional international tax law is designed and interpreted based on the assumption that the various constituent entities or members of an MNE group are independent of each other and conduct transactions with each other at arm's length.

While criticizing the independent entity theory as the fundamental flaw of the existing rules, the BEPS Monitoring Group identified a new but implicit approach in the G20 mandate to treat the corporate group of an MNE as a single firm, and ensure that its tax base is attributed according to its real activities in each country. This means that the new destination of taxing MNEs where economic activities take place and value is created is unlikely to be achieved, without treating the MNE group as a single firm.

I also support the single unitary entity principle. In my view, the G20 mandate could be interpreted as both a new direction and a new guiding philosophy, which requires that all the BEPS Actions should serve the purpose of taxing MNEs where economic activities take place and value is created in the most efficient manner. Guided by the brand new philosophy, the principle of single unitary entity and the basic concepts of residence and source need to be established as the cornerstones to support the design, interpretation, and implementation of new measures in the BEPS package.

Unfortunately, the BEPS project refused to make the implied principle explicit, but has continued to emphasize the independent entity principle, while attempting to counteract its harmful consequences. Consequently, the BEPS outputs fail to provide a coherent and comprehensive approach, and offer instead proposals for a patch-up of existing rules, making them even more contradictory and complex.

According to my observation, virtually all the new rules of the BEPS package are still built on the notional principle of independent entity. By its very nature, the untouchable principle of arm's length ultimately derives from the root of independent entity theory. Additionally, many other flawed rules including weak CFC rule and territorial and deferral systems are also indirectly but closely connected with the independent entity principle.

The orthodoxy of independent entity taxation has two basic assumptions. First, the members of the MNE group are regarded as equal, separate, and independent legal persons. Namely, the members of an MNE group are reasonable legal entities. From the perspective of corporate law, the fiction of independent entity in the context of a corporate group derives from the orthodoxy of shareholder's limited liability and the corporate independent status as legal persons in the traditional corporate law. Second, the contracts between the related parties in the corporate group are freely negotiated at arm's length, and the terms of the contract are fair and reasonable dealings. In short, both the entities and the transactions in the corporate group are reasonable, therefore legal and moral.

However, the two beautiful and attractive assumptions do not make sense, and they do not really exist in the commercial reality. The primary commercial reality is that a multinational corporate group operates more like a single, unitary entity or enterprise rather than separate independent entities or enterprises. This is made possible by the controlling power of the parent corporation. As traditional international tax law stubbornly insists on the old concept of independent entity, the MNEs have been encouraged to incorporate dozens and even hundreds of affiliates all over the world to undertake aggressive BEPS schemes. The more subsidiaries or members in the MNE family, the stronger the parent corporation in reducing the overall transaction cost and advancing the profitability of the group as a whole. Why?

The answer is very simple. All the commercial activities of the subsidiaries and affiliates are under the effectively direct or indirect control of the parent corporation. Therefore, the profits or benefits could be unlimited by separate but coordinated operations of business under the uniform controlling power. On the other hand, the principle of independent entity could better protect the MNEs from unlimited risks and liabilities of group members toward *bona fide* third parties including the tax authorities. Therefore, the legal risks and liabilities of corporate group are limited by law, because there is no joint and several liability between and among the group members unless otherwise agreed by the corporate group members.

Because of the controlling power of the parent corporation on the top of the pyramid of the complicated corporate structure, like a smart spider on the center of a grand network of corporate groups, it is unlikely to find real arm's length transaction in reality. In fact, the related party contracts within the corporate group are always concluded without seriously free, competitive, and transparent bargainings and negotiations.

If the BEPS project is designed on the principle of single unitary entity, the BEPS counter-measure will be much more simple and effective, as inter-group transactions will be disregarded, and the profit or tax base will be attributed to its real activities which generate the profit and create the value in the jurisdictions.

Unfortunately, many actions of the BEPS project, including but not confined to Action 2 on hybrid mismatches, Action 7 on PE, and Actions 8–10 on transferring pricing, heavily rely on the legal fictions of independent entity and arm's length transaction.

11.2.3   The survival and continuity of the problematic benefit principle

The OECD declared that, the goal of the BEPS package is "to tackle BEPS structures by comprehensively addressing their root causes rather than merely the symptoms. Once the measures are implemented, many schemes facilitating double non-taxation will be curtailed".[3] Therefore, a key question is whether all root causes, instead of symptoms, have been addressed?

In my opinion, one of the root causes is traditional benefit principle, which has guided the allocation of global profits in the past decades, and has created many BEPS opportunities. Unfortunately, the BEPS project failed in replacing the benefit principle. Instead, the BEPS package was still designed based on residence jurisdictions for passive income and source jurisdictions for active income.

As articulated in this chapter, my argument is that BEPS concerns will be more effectively tackled if passive income is primarily taxed at source and active income is primarily taxed at residence. This new philosophy will help to build a new international tax governance framework of win–win, which will benefit both developed countries and developing countries. Moreover, the conflicts between the domestic

---

OECD (2015), *Explanatory Statement, OECD/G20 Base Erosion and Profit Shifting Project*, 5.

demand for tax revenue and domestic policy to attract foreign direct investment will be better balanced, and the MNEs and domestic firms will be offered a level playing field.

Many scholars have realized the significance of the renovation of basic principles of current international tax law. As Mindy Herzfeld argued,

> attempts at coordination cannot be successful unless there is agreement on an underlying set of principles for allocating the revenue of global citizens (including natural persons and legal entities). A more rigorous effort to develop such a clear and agreed upon set of principles which rests on economic, philosophic and fairness grounds is needed.[4]

11.2.4   Limited inclusiveness and multilateralism

Global challenges need global solutions. BEPS, as a global concern, is made possible by uncoordinated tax rules at domestic and international levels. Therefore, the global solutions need to be based on inclusive and multilateral global governance. This means that each and every country should be offered equal opportunity and equal weight to shape the outcome of the global solutions.

Although OECD/G20 have made great efforts in organizing many non-member countries and NGOs to participate in the development of the BEPS package, the inclusiveness and multilateralism of the BEPS project is limited for a number of reasons.

First, the undisputed fact is that major OECD countries dominated the formulation of the BEPS package in the process of discussions and negotiations. As OECD countries are all developed countries, it is inevitable that the BEPS project is mainly a result of compromise between the rich countries. For instance, weak measures on CFCs, interest deductibility, and innovation box schemes are favored particularly by the UK.

Second, although over 60 countries were directly involved in the process of the BEPS project, they only account for less than one-third of 193 UN members. As MNEs have their taxable presence around the globe, including the non-participating countries, the effectiveness of

---

4 Mindy Herzfeld, "The Limits of Tax Coordination", working draft, October 11, 2015.

the BEPS project is very limited. The tax competitions between participating countries and non-participating countries will continue. The race to the bottom and the unilateral actions taken by any jurisdiction could hurt all the countries in the world.

Third, although some developing countries were consulted for the BEPS project, it does not necessarily mean that their core proposals were finally accepted by the BEPS package. As observed by independent commentators, some key OECD countries opposed and succeeded in blocking the institutional reform proposal from developing countries at the 3rd International Conference on "Financing for Development".

Fourth, less influential participating countries and more than 120 non-participating counties might be hurt due to the effect of negative spillover arising from the implementation of the BEPS project in the future. They are weak not only because of their limited influence in the renovation of the current rules, but also because of their limited experience and resources to enforce the BEPS Actions.

Fifth, the process of public debate and consulting was relatively insufficient. BEPS Monitoring Group, an active tax justice advocate, complains that they have been vastly outnumbered by the army of paid tax advisers and representatives of multinational enterprises. Although stakeholder interest, including invaluable interactions with business and civil society, saw more than 12,000 pages of comments received on the 23 discussion drafts published and discussed at 11 public consultations, it is unknown to what extent these valuable proposals have been adopted by the BEPS package. More importantly, detailed reasons for rejecting different proposals have not been published.

Given that it is impossible to guarantee that countries and stakeholders really had the equal opportunity to influence and shape the outcome of the BEPS package on genuinely equal footing, OECD and/or G20 is not the truly global platform for comprehensive reform of international tax law. To transform the current BEPS project into truly global, coherent, coordinated, and inclusive actions, the UN should undertake the leadership in the next stage of international tax law reform.

The third paragraph of Article 1 of the Charter of the UN recognizes that the third purpose of the UN is to achieve international cooperation in solving international problems of an economic, social, cultural, or humanitarian character. The fourth paragraph of Article 1 of the

Charter of the UN recognizes its fourth purpose is to "be a centre for harmonizing the actions of nations in the attainment of these common ends".

I believe that the UN will be more qualified, impartial, transparent, credible, and influential than the OECD/G20 in rewriting and renovating the international tax rules including the BEPS counter-measures. All UN members have the right to be heard and represented in the process of international tax law reform. As the working group of the UN, the UN Tax Committee is expected to make a great difference in this regard.

I urge that the UN Convention of Anti-BEPS be made the cornerstone of the global response to BEPS in a more coherent, inclusive, and multilateral manner. Compared with the partial multilateral approach of OEC/G20, the global BEPS Actions launched by the UN will better address concerns about BEPS and restore the integrity of international tax principles of single tax, neutrality, transparency, and fairness.

11.3   Reconsidering the ITR: a multilateral solution

As stated above, in my opinion it is time to re-evaluate the benefits principle. Most of the current issues can be solved if we taxed passive income primarily at source and active income primarily at residence.

For passive income, the number of source jurisdictions is much smaller than residence jurisdictions. Because most individuals are relatively risk-averse, portfolio investment flows overwhelmingly to a small number of countries – the US, the EU, and Japan. If these three jurisdictions could impose a withholding tax on all outbound payments, most of the problem of taxing passive income could be resolved. Crucially, money cannot stay in tax havens and earn decent rates of return, so the cooperation of tax havens in not needed.

In the case of active income, about 90 percent of large multinationals are headquartered in G20 countries, and none of those countries have a corporate tax rate below 20 percent. If the G20 taxed their multinationals (based on where the headquarters are located) on a current basis and restricted the ability to move the headquarters, the problem of taxing active income would be largely resolved as well. This would take care of the Apple and Caterpillar problems, because all of their offshore income would be subject to current US taxation.

As I have argued elsewhere, this multilateral approach takes care of the three common critiques of abolishing deferral of tax on active income. These critiques are based on economic neutrality, competitiveness, and the risk of corporate expatriations. If all our major competitors are subject to the same regime, this resolves all three problems.

But what if the other countries in the G20 are unlikely to coordinate with the US? In that case, the solution is "constructive unilateralism": unilateral action by the US that leads to action by other jurisdictions.

The precedent is the adoption of the CFC rules, which proves (among other examples) that such action can be both possible and effective in pushing other countries to adopt similar rules.

Before 1961, no country taxed the foreign source income of subsidiaries of its multinationals, because residence countries believed they lacked both source and residence jurisdiction over foreign source income of foreign corporations. However, in 1961 the Kennedy Administration proposed taxing all income of CFCs by using a deemed dividend mechanism that was copied from the FPHC (Foreign Personal Holding Company) rules.

While this proposal was rejected, the resulting compromise (Subpart F, 1962) aimed at taxing income of CFCs that was unlikely to be taxed by source countries either because it was mobile and could be earned anywhere (passive income) or because it was structured to be earned in low-tax jurisdictions (base company income).

Initially, the adoption of Subpart F seemed to have put US-based multi-nationals at a competitive disadvantage, because no other country had such rules. But gradually this picture changed. The US was followed by Germany (1972), Canada (1975), Japan (1978), France (1980), United Kingdom (1984), New Zealand (1988), Australia (1990), Sweden (1990), Norway (1992), Denmark (1995), Finland (1995), Indonesia (1995), Portugal (1995), Spain (1995), Hungary (1997), Mexico (1997), South Africa (1997), South Korea (1997), Argentina (1999), Brazil (2000), Italy (2000), Estonia (2000), Israel (2003), Turkey (2006), and China (2008). Many other countries, such as India, are considering adopting such rules. As a result, most of our trading partners now have CFC rules.

Moreover, the later adopters improved on the US in two principal ways. First, they rejected the deemed dividend mechanism, which can lead to many unforeseen complications, in favor of taxing the shareholders on a pass-through basis. Second, in general they explicitly incorporated the effective foreign tax rate into the determination of whether a CFC will be subject to current tax. This is better than the US rule that is based solely on the type of income, because after 1980 it became quite easy to earn active income that is not subject to tax.

The result is that the CFCs of EU-based multinationals are currently generally subject to tax at similar or higher rates than US-based ones, despite the non-taxation of dividends from active income under territoriality. This is therefore a classic example of constructive unilateralism. The US led and others followed, and the end result is that most multinationals are subject to similar effective tax rates, with no competitive disadvantage or advantage. The result is a world in which there is much less double non-taxation than in the absence of CFC rules.

Unfortunately, in the US Subpart F has been critically undermined by the adoption of check the box and the CFC-to-CFC exception, resulting in $2 trillion of low-taxed accumulated earnings offshore by US multinationals. This cannot happen in other countries with tougher CFC rules, and is a major part of the reason why, despite rampant tax competition, most OECD members did not see the sharp drops in overall corporate tax revenues that are seen in developing countries.

The main argument in favor of territoriality (i.e, exempting dividends paid by US CFCs from tax upon receipt by their parents) is the lock-out problem. About $2 trillion in low-taxed foreign source income are in CFCs that cannot repatriate them because of the 35 percent tax on repatriations and the absence of foreign tax credits. We know this is a real problem because of the effectiveness of the 2004–05 amnesty and because of various attempts by multinationals to avoid the rule (e.g., via inversions, "killer Bs", short-term loans, etc.).

But it is less clear that the solution is a participation exemption. Why not abolish deferral and let the dividends flow back tax-free?

I would argue that this is a good opportunity for "constructive unilateralism". No G20 country has a corporate tax rate below 20 percent. If the US reduced the corporate tax to, say, 28 percent, and at the same time abolished deferral, the likely response by other G20 members like Germany or France would be to follow suit. They need the extra revenue more than the US does, and concerns about competitiveness would be alleviated by the US move, like they were in the original CFC context.

It should be remembered that the other G20 have more effective CFC rules than the US, and those CFC rules already act as a de facto world-wide system with a minimum tax: if the foreign tax is below a set level (e.g., 25 percent in Germany or 20 percent in Japan), the CFC rules kick in to tax the income. The result is that there is much less lock-out because most low-taxed foreign income is taxed by the CFC rules. The change to a worldwide system would be much less radical than usually envisaged. This is why for both the UK and Japan there was no significant increase in repatriations after they adopted territoriality in 2009.

But should the US not adopt a minimum but lower tax on foreign source income for competitiveness reasons? This is what both the Obama and Camp proposals envisaged. Obama suggested a 28 percent corporate tax on domestic profits and a 19 percent tax on foreign income, while Camp proposed a 25 percent tax on domestic profits and a 12.5–15 percent tax on foreign income.

The problem, of course, is that such a gap would still encourage US-based MNEs to shift profits overseas, with no repatriation tax to deter them. The US could always fall back to such a system if needed. But for now I would suggest taxing all income at the same rate, and if that rate has to be lower, so be it. As long as it is above 20 percent I do not think the US will be outside G20 norms, and a rate in the 20–25 percent range will not put US MNEs at a significant competitive disadvantage given the effective minimum tax imposed by the CFC rules of its trading partners.

It is impossible to predict what will happen, but the history described above suggests that there is a good chance that other G20 countries would follow the US if it abolished deferral at a lower rate. And if that happened, all the usual objections to worldwide taxation (competitiveness, inversions, and the various neutralities) lose their force. I do not think there is a significant risk involved in this move, and the potential upside is quite large.

11.4   Conclusion

The benefits principle should be reconsidered in light of the reality of globalization. Passive income should be taxed primarily at source and active income primarily at residence. This would enable the large economies to address both individual tax evasion and corporate tax avoidance.

These problems must be addressed if we are to maintain and expand the benefits of globalization. The US public support of globalization hinges on the existence of a social insurance safety net. If the rich and large corporations are not perceived to pay their fair share, the public's willingness to pay tax to support this safety net is eroded. Once a culture of not paying taxes is established, it is very hard to change. We need to do something about both tax evasion and avoidance before it is too late.

12 BEPS, ATAP and the new tax dialogue: a transatlantic competition?

The Tax Cuts and Jobs Act (TRA17) signed into law by President Trump on December 22, 2017 contains multiple provisions that incorporate the principles of the OECD/G20 BEPS into domestic US tax law. Together with the changes in the 2016 US Model Tax Treaty, these provisions mean that the US is following the EU in implementing BEPS and particularly its underlying principle, the single tax principle (all income should be subject to tax once at the rate derived from the benefits principle, i.e., active income at a minimum source tax rate and passive at the residence state rate). This represents a triumph for the G20/OECD and is incongruent with the generally held view that the US will never adopt BEPS.

12.1 Introduction: the US and BEPS

Since the BEPS's launch in 2013, the US has actively participated in all aspects of the project. However, until recently, the general view was that following the conclusion of the BEPS negotiations and the change of Administration, the US was stepping back from the BEPS process. While the EU was charging ahead with implementing BEPS through the Anti-Tax Avoidance Directive (ATAD), the US stated that it was already in compliance with all BEPS minimum standards and therefore other than country-by-country reporting (CbCR) it had no further BEPS obligations. The US decided not to sign the Multilateral Convention to Implement Tax Treaty Related Measures to Prevent Base Erosion and Profit Shifting (MLI), which would have obliged it to implement BEPS into tax treaties and did not join the CRS to further automatic exchange of information, leading the EU to call it a tax haven. The US has adopted BEPS provisions in its model tax treaty but these provisions have not been implemented in an actual US treaty. Thus, most observers believe that the US has abandoned the BEPS effort.

This view is not wholly correct. The current tax reform legislation clearly relies on BEPS principles and particularly on the single tax principle. This represents a triumph for the G20/OECD and challenges the opinion that the US will never adopt BEPS.

This chapter proceeds in four parts. Sections 12.2, 12.3 and 12.4. analyze the three BEPS provisions included in TRA17: a one-time "transition tax" on untaxed accumulated earnings and profits (E&P) of certain non-US corporations (new section 965) and two anti-base erosion and income shifting provisions, namely a foreign minimum tax on 10 percent US shareholders of CFCs to the extent the CFCs are treated as having GILTI (new section 951A) and a base erosion and anti-abuse tax (BEAT) that will be imposed in relation to deductible payments made by certain corporations to their non-US affiliates (new section 59A). Section 12.5 discusses one of the key BEPS Action items that caused the most concern in the US, i.e. Action 6 on the prevention of treaty abuse through inclusion of a principal purpose test (PPT). In section 12.6, the authors argue that Congress could have done more, especially with regard to the anti-hybrid rules for certain related-party amounts of the new section 267A since it does not have any significant impact on foreign-to-foreign hybrid planning. To this extent, it should be noted that in order to limit the application of Subpart F exceptions to transactions that use reverse hybrids to create *stateless income*, the Obama Administration proposed a rule that would provide that sections 954(c) and 954(c)(6) do not apply to payments made to a foreign reverse hybrid held directly by a US owner when those amounts are treated as deductible payments received from foreign related persons. Section 12.7 provides some conclusions.

12.2 Past accumulations

Section 965 of TRA17 provides for a one-time deemed repatriation tax on previously untaxed accumulated foreign earnings. TRA17 splits E&P between cash and illiquid assets with cash amounts taxed at a 15.5 percent effective rate and illiquid assets taxed at an 8 percent effective rate. The taxpayer may elect to pay this tax over an eight-year period. However, if a US shareholder becomes an "expatriated entity" within the meaning of section 7874(a)(2) at any point within the ten-year period following enactment of TRA17, the benefits of the reduced rates would be recaptured. In that event, the US shareholder would be subject to an additional tax equal to 35 percent of the amount of the deduction allowed in respect of the transition tax. No foreign tax credits are permitted to offset this additional tax.

The accumulation of offshore profits by US multinationals in low-tax jurisdictions has been the focus of significant concern and a primary driver of the BEPS effort. The EU ATAD and State aid as well as the UK's DPT and current discussion on the digital economy all reflect these concerns. Indeed, these earnings, accumulated since the 2004–05 tax amnesty and currently exceeding $2.6 trillion, are located in just seven low-tax jurisdictions and they are highly concentrated: just four companies (Apple, Microsoft, Pfizer, and GE) hold approximately one-quarter (24 percent) of the offshore profits. Ten companies have 38 percent of the profits and 50 companies hold three-quarters of the earnings.

In my opinion, there are four reasons why such low rates are inappropriate for past earnings. First, as a policy matter, there is no justification for not taxing these profits in full, because they do not raise competitiveness issues (since they have been earned) or behavioural response issues (since the behaviour has already happened), and because they mostly represent earnings on IP developed in the US with hefty taxpayer support.

Second, there are a few outstanding issues with dual rates, including: (a) what may be considered a "cash or cash equivalent" for the purposes of this tax, and (b) whether there would be a look-back rule for "cash or cash equivalent" assets recently invested to take advantage of the lower rate, or a more general anti-abuse rule targeting transactions carried out to achieve the lower rate. The reason is simple: taxpayers are incentivized to manipulate their foreign cash positions by converting cash to more illiquid investments and by legitimately distributing some of their cash through dividend payments or other means. The new law includes both a look-back rule and a subjective intent-based anti-abuse test, the PPT. Indeed, section 965(c)(3)(A) provides a formula for calculating how much E&P should be attributed to cash assets and therefore subject to the higher 15.5 percent rate. The benchmark is the "aggregate foreign cash position" calculated as the greater of either

the pro rata share of the cash position of all specified foreign corporations as of the last day of the last taxable year beginning before January 1, 2018, or the average of the cash position determined on the last day of each of the two taxable years ending immediately before November 2, 2017.

In addition, section 965(c)(3)(F) states that, "If the Secretary determines that *a principal purpose* of any transaction was to reduce the aggregate foreign cash position taken into account under this subsection, such transaction shall be disregarded for purposes of this subsection" (emphasis added). The Conference Report accompanying TRA17, states that, "The provision also authorizes the Secretary to disregard transactions that are determined to have *the principal purpose* of reducing the aggregate foreign cash position" (emphasis added), thus, viewing those two formulations as having the same meaning. But if "a principal purpose" shall be defined as being one of its "first-in-importance" purposes, I believe that the effectiveness of section 965(c)(3)(F) would be substantially undermined. In this regard, the extensive report prepared by the Tax Section of the New York State Bar Association on the 1994 proposed partnership anti-abuse regulation stated:

> If a transaction were subject to attack only if 'the' principal purpose were tax avoidance, the result would be a substantially increased willingness on the part of taxpayers to engage in aggressive transactions. In our experience, a taxpayer usually is able to assert some nontax purpose for a transaction, even if that purpose is on its face borderline. *Any such claim would have to satisfy a much lower threshold of "believability"* if the test were whether "the" principal purpose of the transaction is tax avoidance ... The history of § 269, the corporate anti-abuse rule that applies only when "the" principal purpose of a transaction is tax avoidance, demonstrates the weakness of such a test. The Service has been unable to successfully apply § 269 with any regularity, as indicated by the dearth of judicial decisions under that section as well as our experience that agents in the field rarely attempt to apply the section. We believe those results may be attributable to § 269's requirement that "the" principal purpose of a transaction be tax avoidance, which *often allows the taxpayer to prevail by asserting a relatively weak business purpose.*[1]

Third, studies have highlighted that repatriated earnings in 2004 were used to send cash back to shareholders, either in the form of dividends or stock buybacks, instead of being invested in new US jobs and infrastructure as President Trump sold TRA17 on the promise that,

> *the plan is going to bring trillions of dollars back into the United States, money that's offshore* ... But you look at the great companies – Apple and so

---

1 *NYSBA Submits Report on Partnership Antiabuse Regulation* (July 1, 1994) (Doc 94-6234) 94 TNT 130-34, (emphasis added).

many others. They have billions of dollars overseas that they want to bring back. Now they're going to be able to bring it back, and we'll [*sic*] spending that money, and they'll be spending that money right here. *And it will be jobs and lots of other good things.*[2]

Thus, it is highly likely that repatriated funds will be used for already planned projects, such as pay down existing borrowings, setting off a new wave of mergers and acquisitions, rather than being invested in expansion. For example, Cisco expects to spend much of the newly repatriated cash on share buybacks and dividends over the next two years. On the other hand, Apple announced in January 2018 that it would invest $30 billion in capital spending in the US; over five years that would create more than 20,000 jobs. However, analysts questioned whether Apple's commitments were new and impacted in any way by the tax reform, since the company would have been able to make this investment with existing cash flow – without needing to tap into cash holdings.

Last but not least, this money is not trapped offshore. Under the previous section 956(c)(2)(A) and (F), a foreign subsidiary's untaxed earnings might have been invested without triggering the deemed dividend rules regarding stock of a domestic corporation, a debt obligation of a US person, or a US bank deposit, as long as the issuer was not a US shareholder or did not have a 25 percent or other proscribed relationship with the foreign subsidiary. The US Senate Permanent Subcommittee on Investigations on the 2004 tax holiday has shown that at the end of FY2010, of the $538 billion in undistributed accumulated foreign earnings of 20 US multinational corporations, nearly half (46 percent) of the funds that the corporations had identified as offshore and for which US taxes had been deferred were actually deposited in the names of CFCs in accounts at US financial institutions. Recent data compiled by Bloomberg shows that the top ten US multinationals have boosted their investments in government bonds to $113 billion from $67 billion and have received at least $1.4 billion in interest payments over the past five years.

---

2 Remarks by President Trump at Lunch with Bicameral Tax Conferees, Budget & Spending (13 Dec. 2017), available at www.whitehouse.gov/briefings-statements/remarks-president-trump-lunch-bicameral-tax-conferees/ (accessed 5 Apr. 2018) (emphasis added).

12.3   Future accumulations

In TRA17, the shift from a worldwide system of taxation to a quasi-territorial one is accompanied by some sort of a foreign minimum tax, the so-called GILTI provision, the *stick*. The intent is to discourage erosion of the US base by moving or holding intangible assets outside the US. Under the new section 951A(a), a US shareholder of any CFC must include in its gross income for a taxable year its GILTI in a manner generally similar to inclusion of Subpart F income. GILTI means, with respect to any US shareholder for the shareholder's taxable year, the excess (if any) of the shareholder's net CFC tested income over the shareholder's net deemed tangible income return. Net deemed tangible income return is, for a US shareholder for a taxable year, the excess (if any) of 10 percent of the aggregate of its pro rata share of the qualified business asset investment (QBAI) of each CFC with respect to which it is a US shareholder over the amount of interest expense taken into account in determining its net CFC tested income for the taxable year, to the extent that the interest expense exceeds the interest income properly allocable to the interest expense that is taken into account in determining its net CFC tested income. Net CFC tested income means, for a US shareholder, the excess of the aggregate of the shareholder's pro rata share of the tested income of each CFC with respect to which it is a US shareholder, over the aggregate of its pro rata share of the tested loss of each CFC with respect to which it is a US shareholder. The tested income of a CFC means the excess (if any) of the gross income of the corporation – determined without regard to certain exceptions to tested income – over deductions (including taxes) properly allocable to such gross income. QBAI means, with respect to any CFC for a taxable year, the average of the aggregate of its adjusted bases, determined as of the close of each quarter of the taxable year, in specified tangible property used in its trade or business and of a type with respect to which a deduction is generally allowable under section 167. To put it simply, the formula for GILTI can be expressed as:

GILTI = Net CFC tested income – [(10 percent x QBAI) – interest
      expense]

As a result, the formula generally exempts from inclusion a deemed return on tangible assets and assumes the residual income to be intangible income that is subject to current US tax.

The tax rate for future GILTI is determined by taking the 21 percent corporate tax rate and allowing a deduction of 50 percent, to give a net rate of 10.5 percent. This rate can be partially offset by foreign tax credits but in a separate basket (but with cross-averaging within the basket). The provision is effective for taxable years of foreign corporations beginning after 31 December 2017.

What this means in plain English is that Amazon, Apple, Facebook, Google, Netflix and their ilk will have to pay tax at 10.5 percent on future GILTI because they have CFCs that produce "tested income" (and no loss) in excess of 10 percent over their basis in offshore tangible assets, which will be zero or close to it (since they derive almost all of their income from intangibles). Other MNEs (e.g. GE or Intel) will pay less because they have more tangible assets offshore. This creates an obvious incentive to move jobs (not just profits) offshore. In this regard, a Baker McKenzie Client Alert observed that,

> the GILTI rules create a surprising and unexpected incentive for U.S. multinationals to increase the amount of tangible assets held by their CFCs, which in most circumstances will presumably be situated outside the United States. Assuming a more or less steady amount of overall income potentially subject to Section 951A (and deductible under Section 250), increasing QBAI held by CFCs may be one of the most effective ways to manage or reduce GILTI.[3]

To address these issues, TRA17 proposes two solutions. First, section 951A(d)(4) includes a very broad anti-abuse provision which reads as follows:

> [f]or purposes of determining QBAI, the Secretary is authorized to issue anti-avoidance regulations or other guidance as the Secretary determines appropriate, including regulations or other guidance that provide for the treatment of property if the property is transferred or held temporarily, or *if avoidance was a factor* in the transfer or holding of the property. [emphasis added]

Second, section 250(a)(1)(A) provides a 37.5 percent FDII, the *carrot*, with the result that the portion of a US corporation's intangible income derived from serving foreign markets is effectively taxed at 13.125

---

3   Baker McKenzie, *Tax News and Developments – Client Alert* (20 Dec. 2017), at p. 21, available at www.bakermckenzie.com/-/media/files/insight/publications/2017/12/client-alert--us-tax-ref orm--the-tax-cuts-and-jobs-act-congress-passe.pdf?la=en (accessed 5 Apr. 2018).

percent. The intent is to encourage US multinationals to remain in the country and keep their assets, earnings, jobs, and functions there.

Section 250(b)(1) defines the FDII of any domestic corporation as the amount which bears the same ratio to the corporation's "deemed intangible income" as its "foreign-derived deduction eligible" income bears to its "deduction eligible income". In other words, a domestic corporation's FDII is its deemed intangible income multiplied by the percentage of its deduction eligible income that is foreign-derived.

Deemed intangible income is the excess of a domestic corporation's deduction eligible income over its deemed tangible income return.

The "foreign-derived deduction eligible income" is defined as income derived in connection with (a) property that is sold by the taxpayer to any foreign person for a foreign use, or (b) services provided to any foreign person, or with respect to foreign property. Foreign use means any use, consumption, or disposition which is not within the US. For purposes of the provision, the terms "sold", "sells", and "sale" include any lease, exchange, or other disposition.

Special rules for determining foreign use apply to transactions that involve property or services provided to domestic intermediaries or related parties. Section 250(b)(5)(B) and (b)(5)(C) operate to make sure that property is ultimately sold to a foreign person for use or consumption abroad, or services are provided to a person, or with respect to property, located outside the US. If property is sold to a related foreign party, the sale is not treated as for foreign use unless the property is sold by the related foreign party to another person who is unrelated and is not a US person, and the taxpayer establishes to the satisfaction of the Secretary that such property is for a foreign use. Transactions implicating this rule might arise where, for example, a US corporate taxpayer who owns IP rights domestically in film or television programming licenses those rights to a wholly owned foreign subsidiary, which, in turn, sub-licenses the content in its local market to third parties. A similar restriction also exists with services provided to a related party located outside the US. Income derived from such a transaction does not qualify as foreign-derived deduction eligible income unless the taxpayer establishes to the satisfaction of the Secretary that the service is not substantially similar to services provided by the related party to persons located within the US.

There are three obvious problems with the FDII deduction.

According to a group of 13 tax law professors, taxpayers may be able to take advantage of the reduced rate on export income through "resale" transactions where goods are sold to independent foreign distributors who subsequently resell back into the US. In their opinion, Treasury should address such "roundtripping" transactions in regulations with rules similar to those under Treas. Reg. 1.954-3(a)(3)(ii), which determine the place of use, consumption, or disposition of property for foreign base company sales income purposes. In particular, Treasury should require US manufacturers to conduct a real investigation of how much the independent foreign party will sell back into the US.

Another major issue that Treasury should focus on is the level of further processing required to qualify as foreign use. Assuming that roundtripping transactions are permitted to the extent that the property sold is somewhat further processed abroad, what would be the minimum amount of further processing necessary to allow reimportation into the US? In my opinion, Treasury should apply standards similar to the "substantial transformation" and/or "substantial contribution" tests provided by Treas. Reg. 1.954-3(a)(4)(ii) and 1.954-3(a)(4)(iv). If substantial transformation and/or contribution may sound like high standards, I believe that property should be, at least, significantly or materially modified before being reimported into the US. Additional guidance will be needed for computer software transactions where software is licensed to be merely imprinted in physical CDs and then sold back into the US. In my opinion, income derived from such a transaction should not qualify as foreign-derived deduction eligible income since the software is merely imprinted in physical form and not significantly modified.

Second, I believe that the FDII regime is clearly inconsistent with the modified nexus approach adopted by the OECD in the BEPS because it does not require any activity to be carried out in the US other than exporting. Taxpayers can receive the lower rate by importing goods and immediately exporting them. As stated by Schler,

> the provision does not require that anything be manufactured in the U.S. The formula is based only on profits from exports. A U.S. corporation could buy goods from a related or unrelated foreign supplier, resell them around the world, and have FDII for its profits on foreign sales. Not a single employee need be in the United States.[4]

---

4 M.L. Schler, "Reflections on the Pending Tax Cut and Jobs Act", *Tax Forum* 686 (4 Dec. 2017), 41.

Third, the FDII regime has a blatant and obvious WTO problem: it is a subsidy contingent upon export performance, which is explicitly prohibited by Article 3.1(a) of the Subsidies and Countervailing Measures Agreement (SCM). This was precisely the type of export subsidy struck down in the *Domestic International Sales Corporation, Foreign Sales Corporation* and *Extraterritorial Income* cases, resulting in massive potential sanctions and forcing the US to repeal the subsidy and enact a domestic manufacturing provision (section 199) that did not violate the SCM because it was not contingent upon export performance. The FDII has a very low chance of surviving a WTO dispute, not only because it clearly satisfies the definition of a "prohibited subsidy" under the SCM agreement, but also because it is inconsistent with the main arguments advanced by the US during the US–FSC litigation. I would expect that this provision will be struck down by the WTO and the US will be left with only the GILTI provision. As stated above, the GILTI provision is inadequate but this can be fixed by a future Democratic Administration if the GILTI rate is set as the same as the domestic rate (21 percent).

12.4   Base erosion

The Conference Agreement followed the Senate's BEAT with some changes, an alternative to the House excise tax proposal. Under the new section 59A(a), an "applicable taxpayer" is required to pay a tax equal to the "base erosion minimum tax amount" for the taxable year. The BEAT generally applies to corporations (other than regulated investments companies, (RICs), real estate investment trusts (REITs) or S corporations) that over a three-year period have average annual gross receipts of at least $500 million and a "base erosion percentage" for the taxable year of at least 3 percent. The "base erosion minimum tax amount" is the excess of 10 percent of the taxpayer's "modified taxable income" over the taxpayer's "regular tax liability" (defined in section 26(b)) reduced (but not below zero) by the excess (if any) of credits allowed against such regular tax liability over the sum of: (a) section 38 credit properly allocable to the section 41(a) research credit; plus (b) the portion of the applicable section 38 credits not in excess of 80 percent of the lesser of the amount of such credits or the base erosion minimum tax amount.

To determine its modified taxable income, a corporation computes its taxable income for the year without regard to any base erosion tax benefit with respect to any base erosion payment or the base erosion percentage of any allowable net operating loss deduction allowed under section 172 for the taxable year. A base erosion payment is defined as any amount paid or accrued to a foreign related person that is a related party of the taxpayer and with respect to which a deduction is allowable, including interest and royalties; amounts paid in connection with an acquisition of property subject to the allowance of depreciation (or amortization in lieu of depreciation); premiums or other consideration paid or accrued for any reinsurance payments and, for inverted corporations only, also the COGS. On the other hand, payments for services if such services qualify for the services cost method under Treas. Reg. section 1.482-9 and only if they are made for services that have no mark-up component, as well as any qualified derivative payment, are not treated as base erosion payments.

A couple of preliminary observations are in order. First, the real purpose of BEAT seems to be somehow ambiguous and confounding. If BEAT intends to prevent the erosion of and protect the US tax base, why does it make a distinction between payments to foreign related parties and payments to unrelated ones, and include only the former in calculating the new tax? Stevens and Barnes[5] argue that the definition of base erosion payment apparently reflects the US government's lack of confidence in policing transfer pricing. In this regard, it should be noted that section 59A(i) provides that the Secretary of the Treasury is to prescribe such regulations or other guidance necessary or appropriate, including regulations providing for such adjustments to the application of this section necessary to prevent avoidance of the provision, including through: (a) the use of *unrelated persons, conduit transactions* or *other intermediaries,* or (b) transactions or arrangements designed in whole or in part: (i) to characterize payments otherwise subject to this provision as payments not subject to this provision, or (ii) to substitute payments not subject to this provision for payments otherwise subject to this provision. In the my opinion, principles similar to those under the anti-conduit regulations may be applied to identify whether a foreign related party is the actual beneficial owner of a base erosion payment.

---

5   E.J. Stevens and P.A. Barnes, "Insight: BEAT Strikes the Wrong Note", 53 BNA *Daily Tax Report* 16 (19 Mar. 2018), 2, available at http://www.capdale.com/files/22787_insight_beat_strikes_ thewrong_note.pdf (accessed 5 Apr. 2018): "The only sustainable argument for the BEAT tax is that U.S. transfer pricing enforcement is so wholly ineffectual that it must be backstopped by an automatic penalty on most cross-border related party transactions and a crude proxy for an arm's length price."

Second, BEAT offers tax planning opportunities with unintended consequences. Rather than manufacturing the goods itself and paying the foreign affiliate a royalty for the use of software, trademark, or other intellectual property, a US corporation may prefer to purchase the finished products from a foreign affiliate. The fact that a royalty payment is excluded from a US company's COGS but included in the expanded tax base creates incentives to move jobs offshore.

Finally, can the BEAT be seen as violating the non-discrimination provision of Article 24? Article 24 has two relevant provisions: Article 24(4) and (5). Under Article 24(4),

> *Except where the provisions of paragraph 1 of Article 9* (Associated Enterprises), paragraph 8 of Article 11 (Interest), or paragraph 7 of Article 12 (Royalties) apply, interest, royalties, and other disbursements paid by an enterprise of a Contracting State to a resident of the other Contracting State shall, *for the purpose of determining the taxable profits of such enterprise*, be deductible *under the same conditions* as if they had been paid to a resident of the first-mentioned Contracting State. Similarly, any debts of an enterprise of a Contracting State to a resident of the other Contracting State shall, for the purpose of determining the taxable capital of the first-mentioned resident, be deductible under the same conditions as if they had been contracted to a resident of the first-mentioned Contracting State. [emphasis added]

Does the BEAT violate this provision? I have already argued elsewhere it does not because the BEAT is not equivalent to the denial of a deduction. Interest, royalties, and the other items covered by the BEAT remain fully deductible. Instead, the tax benefit conferred by deducting them is subject to the 10 percent BEAT. The non-equivalence of the BEAT and denying the deduction can be seen from the fact that denying a deduction would increase the tax on the deductible item by 21 percent, not by 10 percent.

In addition, the BEAT can be seen as conceptually similar to a broadly applied thin capitalization rule. In fact, the BEAT replaces the old earnings stripping rule (former IRC section 163(j)). And thin capitalization rules, even though they do frequently involve denying the interest deduction for interest paid to foreign but not domestic related parties, are widely used and generally regarded by the OECD as non-discriminatory.

The other relevant provision of Article 24 is paragraph 5, which states that a country may not apply less favorable treatment to any entity owned or controlled by non-residents in comparison with domestically held entities.

Arguably, this paragraph is violated by the BEAT because a foreign-owned US party will be subject to the BEAT but a US-owned one will not. But there are two counter-arguments. First, the BEAT applies regardless of the ultimate ownership of the US corporation and thus also to payments from a US party to a foreign party that is owned by the US party (e.g. a CFC), which shows that one of the intentions was to protect the US corporate tax base, not to discriminate against foreign-owned US parties.

Second, I have argued that the foreign related party and the US related party are not comparable for applying a non-discrimination analysis. The reason is that the US knows that a US related party is in fact subject to tax on the relevant deductible items, such as interest, royalties, and in some cases, COGS. But the US does not know that the foreign related party is similarly subjected to tax by its country of residence because in many cases these countries will not tax, particularly when it comes to foreign-source interest or royalties. It should be expected that the enactment of the BEAT would lead multinationals to establish related parties that receive deductible payments from US parties precisely in those jurisdictions that exempt such payments, because otherwise they would risk double taxation since a credit would normally not be immediately available.

The guiding spirit behind the international provisions of the TRA17 is the single tax principle, and under that principle it is perfectly appropriate for the US to deny a deduction for items that it has no reason to believe will be taxed on a residence basis. No violation of Article 24(5) should arise under those circumstances. Therefore, rather than engaging in retaliatory actions, EU treaty partners should adopt similar measures and apply them to US multinationals.

12.5   BEPS Action 6: should the US reconsider the rejection of the PPT?

One of the key BEPS Actions that generated the most controversy in the US and eventually led the country not to join the MLI was Action 6, primarily due to the inclusion of a general anti-abuse rule based on the principal purposes of transactions or arrangements (the PPT rule). Under that rule, if one of the principal purposes of transactions or arrangements is to obtain treaty benefits, these benefits will be denied unless it is established that to grant them would be in accordance with the object and purpose of the provisions of the treaty. In order to understand why the US opposed this subjective intention-based test and preferred a more objective detailed LOB provision, which has been part of its treaty policy since 1981, it is necessary to go back to the beginning of the twenty-first century when the US Senate refused to approve the ratification of negotiated treaties with Italy and Slovenia that originally contained a "main purpose" clause.

The Italian negotiators wanted to include a very broad anti-abuse provision which would have denied treaty benefits in situations not covered by the LOB clause. At that time (from 1995 to 2000), Italy did not have effective domestic anti-abuse rules, which could have been used to deny treaty benefits in the case of abusive transactions, and was therefore increasingly relying on explicit anti-abuse provisions in its treaties. Indeed, Italian domestic anti-abuse provisions were so weak that in three cases of the early 2000s, the tax authorities tried unsuccessfully to fight dividend washing transactions through the principle of *fraude à la loi* set forth by Article 1344 of the Civil Code. In particular, Italian negotiators wanted to incorporate a provision similar to Article 30 of the 1995 treaty with Israel, which reads as follows:

> The competent authorities of the Contracting States, upon their mutual agreement, may deny the benefits of this Convention to any person, or with respect to any transaction, if in their opinion the receipt of those benefits, under the circumstances, would constitute an abuse of the Convention according to its purposes.

However, in a hearing before the US Senate Committee on Foreign Relations, Phil West, International Tax Counsel for the US Department of the Treasury, declared that this broad, subjective anti-abuse rule in the Israel-Italy treaty was rejected for several reasons:

> First, it provided a less certain standard against which a taxpayer could meaningfully evaluate its transaction. Second, since the narrower rule ["main purpose" test] before you appears in a significant number of treaties around the world, and promises to appear in more, it is more consistent with international norms and will likely be the subject of more interpretive law than the other standards ...

We gravitated toward the "main purpose" standard of our proposed rule because it corresponds to the U.S. "a principal purpose" standard which is applied in a number of our statutory provisions and regulations.[6]

A compromise was thus reached on the inclusion of the main purpose clause in Articles 10 (Dividends), 11(9) (Interest), 12(8) (Royalties) and 22(3) (Other Income). Article 10(10) of the 1999 treaty with Italy provided that:

> The provisions of this Article shall not apply if it was the main purpose or one of the main purposes of any person concerned with the creation or assignment of the shares or other rights in respect of which the dividend is paid to take advantage of this Article by means of that creation or assignment.

Lindy Paull, Chief of Staff of the Joint Committee on Taxation, told the US Senate Committee on Foreign Relations that:

> While the main purpose tests are intended to prevent inappropriate benefits under the treaty, such tests inject considerable uncertainty into the treaty provisions because such tests are subjective and vague. This uncertainty can create difficulties for legitimate business transactions, and can hinder a taxpayer's ability to rely on the treaty.[7]

The US Senate Committee on Foreign Relations, in turn, stated that the inclusion of such tests represented a fundamental shift in US treaty policy, which was based on clear, bright-line objective tests (such as ownership and base erosion tests, and public company tests, as well as active business tests). In this regard, the Committee complained that it had not been afforded an opportunity to weigh the relevant policy considerations. Accordingly, the Committee placed a reservation on the main purpose test, citing subjectivity, vagueness, and uncertainty as sources of the serious concerns about the provision. The reservation had the effect of striking the objectionable provision from the instrument of ratification.

In my opinion, Phil West's memorandum to Senator Hagel (R-NE) appears to be contradictory while seeking to give meaning to the term

---

6 Testimony before the Senate Committee on Foreign Relations Hearing on Tax Treaties and Protocols with Eight Countries (25 Oct. 1999), JCX-76-99, 4.

7 *Ibid.*

"a principal purpose". On the one hand, West cited Judge Posner's ruling in *Santa Fe Pacific Corporation v. Central States, Southeast and Southwest Areas Pension Fund*, a labour law case governed by the Employee Retirement Income Security Act rules. On the other hand, he listed section 877(a)(2) among the IRC provisions using "a/one of the principal purposes" anti-abuse language. First, *Santa Fe* was not a tax case and did not interpret any provisions of the IRC. Second, its conclusions totally oppose those of several judicial decisions involving sections 367 and 877. *Santa Fe* might have caused enough confusion to lead the Senate to reject the inclusion of the main purpose test in the tax treaties with Italy and Slovenia.

Under the Multiemployer Pension Plan Amendments Act of 1980, an employer that withdrew from a multiemployer pension plan could have been required to pay the plan a sum equal to the vested but unfunded benefits of the employer's employees. The purpose was to avoid situations where the other employers would have had to pay for those benefits. A parent and its subsidiaries were considered to be a single employer with the consequence that if a subsidiary withdrew from the plan, its withdrawal liability could have been assessed against the parent. But in the event that the parent had sold its subsidiary, the parent would not have been liable for withdrawal liability unless a principal purpose of the transaction was to "evade or avoid" parental liability. In determining whether a principal purpose of *Santa Fe* was to evade or avoid its parental liability, the Court held:

> The imposition of withdrawal liability in a sale of business situation requires only that *a* principal purpose of the sale be to escape withdrawal liability. It needn't be the only purpose; it need only have been one of the factors that weighed heavily in the seller's thinking. We can find no decisions discussing situations in which there is more than one principal (major, weighty, salient, important) purpose, but we would be doing violence to the language and the purpose of the statute if we read "a principal" as "the principal." The clear import of "a principal" is to let the employer off the hook even if one of his purposes was to beat withdrawal liability, provided however that it was a minor, subordinate purpose, as distinct from a major purpose. To let the employer off even if avoiding such liability was a major purpose would ill serve the statute's goal of preventing one employer from unloading his pension obligations onto the other employers in a multiemployer plan.[8]

---

8 *Santa Fe Pacific Corp. v. Central States, Southeast and Southwest Areas Pension Fund*, CAFC, Seventh Cir., 22 Apr. 1994, 22 F.3d 725, 73 A.F.T.R.2d 94-1820, 62 USLW 2703, 726–7.

However, such interpretation of the term "a principal purpose" con-trasts starkly with settled case law involving IRC provisions, such as sections 367 and 877. As mentioned above, Phil West adopted Judge Posner's interpretation of the term "a principal purpose" while, at the same time, making reference to section 877 as one of the many Code provisions which contains such language. A 1984 Tax Court case, regarding whether the petitioner had tax avoidance as one of her prin-cipal purposes in expatriating, clearly illustrates West's inconsistency.

Until August 20, 1996, when it was amended by the Health Insurance Portability and Accountability Act (P.L. 104–191, section 511(g)), sec-tion 877 generally provided that a non-resident alien individual who lost his US citizenship should be subject to tax on his US-source income, for the ten-year period following such loss, at the graduated tax rates applicable to US citizens rather than more favorable rates applicable to non-resident aliens, unless the loss did not have as one of its principal purposes the avoidance of US taxes. Section 877(e) specifi-cally assigned the burden of proving the lack of a tax avoidance motive to the expatriate if the respondent established that it was reasonable to believe that the individual's loss of US citizenship would result in a substantial reduction in taxes. In *Furstenberg v. Commissioner*, the taxpayer was able to carry her burden under section 877(e). Furstenberg was the daughter of Robert Lee Blaffer, one of the founders of Humble Oil & Refining Co., the predecessor of Exxon Corporation. Because of the financial success of her father, the petitioner travelled extensively with her family, visiting Europe, in particular, France, where she spent several summers. By the time of her expatriation (December 23, 1975), she was divorced from her second husband, Richard M. Sheridan, an international executive of Mobil Oil Corporation. The genesis for the expatriation was her third marriage to Prince Tassillo von Furstenberg (October 17, 1975), a member of the Austrian aristocracy, whose ances-tors were princes of the Holy Roman Empire in 1664. At the time of their decision to marry in early 1975, Furstenberg explained to the peti-tioner how important it was to him, given his Austrian heritage and ties, that she should have adopted Austrian citizenship. Prior to expatriat-ing, she met with her accountant and informed him that she intended to marry Furstenberg, adopt Austrian citizenship, and live with her husband in Paris. He told her that adopting Austrian nationality would "complicate" her taxes and warned that French taxes could be very high.

The petitioner had no further discussions with her accountant in 1975. Her income in 1975 and 1976 came from two trust distributions she received and from the sale of securities. The distribution from Trust No. 1, a complex inter vivos trust established by her parents, occurred on the day of her expatriation. In addition, in 1976 and 1977, after her expatriation she sold various securities realizing net capital gains in the amounts of $2,601,680,06 and $7,219,440,35 respectively. After careful consideration of all the evidence, the court was convinced that tax avoidance was not one of her principal purposes in expatriating. Interestingly, the Tax Court held the following:

> Although we have never specifically interpreted the phrase "one of its prin-cipal purposes" in the context of section 877, we find instructive the follow-ing definition set forth in *Dittler Bros, Inc. v. Commissioner*, 72 T.C. 896, 915 (1979), affd. without published opinion 642 F.2d 1211 (5th Cir. 1981), in which the Court was called upon to determine, under section 367, whether or not a certain translation was "in pursuance of a plan having as one of its principal purposes the avoidance of Federal income tax."[9]

The Court then quoted the definition of the term "principal purpose" as articulated in *Dittler Bros.*, according to which:

> the term [principal purpose] should be construed in accordance with its ordinary meaning. Such a rule of statutory construction has been endorsed by the *Supreme Court. Malat v. Riddell*, 383 U.S. 569, 571 (1966). Webster's New Collegiate Dictionary defines "principal" as "first in rank, authority, importance, or degree." Thus, the proper inquiry hereunder is whether the exchange of manufacturing know-how was in pursuance of a plan having as one of its *"first-in-importance"* purposes the avoidance of Federal income taxes.[10]

To better understand the logic of Furstenberg's conclusions, it is necessary to closely examine *Dittler Brothers, Inc. v. Commissioner of Internal Revenue*, which interpreted the term "principal purpose" within the context of section 367.

Prior to the Deficit Reduction Act of 1984, section 367(a)(1) provided that certain outbound transfers of appreciated property would be non-taxable only if the exchange did not have the avoidance of Federal income taxes as one of its principal purposes. This determination was

---

9 *Furstenberg v. Commissioner of Internal Revenue*, USTC, 26 Nov. 1984, 83 T.C. No. 43, 83 T.C. 755, Tax Ct. Rep. (CCH) 41, 633, 775–6.

10 *Ibid.*

made by the IRS in accordance with guidelines set out in Rev. Proc. 68-23, 1968-1 C.B. 821. Section 1042(d) of the Tax Reform Act of 1976 afforded taxpayers a remedy through a declaratory judgment procedure in the Tax Court in cases where the IRS issued an adverse ruling or failed to make a determination as to whether a transfer had tax avoidance as a principal purpose. However, the scope of a Tax Court declaratory judgment was limited as to whether the IRS acted reasonably.

In *Dittler Bros.*, the taxpayer had special know-how and trade secrets regarding the manufacturing of "rub-off" lottery tickets. In order to expand its sales into foreign markets, Dittler entered into a 50–50 joint venture with a UK holding company, known as Norton & Wright Group Ltd. (NWG), which had developed a substantial market for the sale of lottery tickets. Dittler had previously granted two non-exclusive licences of its secret process to foreign companies, but since only nominal royalties were produced, both licences were cancelled. Dittler and NWG created two Netherlands Antilles corporations. NWG's representatives requested the joint venture to be located there primarily due to potential tax benefits: a low rate of Netherlands Antilles tax plus Netherlands tax exemption for dividends received. The first corporation, known as Stansfield Security N.V. (SSNV), was owned 50 percent by Dittler and 50 percent by Norton & Wright (Holland) BV (NWBV), NWG's wholly owned Netherlands subsidiary. The second corporation, known as Opax Lotteries International N.V. (OLINV), was wholly owned by SSNV. Dittler and NWBV each contributed $25,000 to SSNV as partial consideration for their respective 50 percent stock interest. In addition, Dittler transferred its secret process for the printing of rub-off tickets to SSNV while NWBV transferred, along with its cash contribution, specific marketing and customer information. Subsequently, SSNV transferred 80 percent of its cash, the manufacturing know-how, and the marketing information to OLINV for 100 percent of its stock.

This contribution qualified SSNV as an investment holding company under Netherlands Antilles law. Under the terms of a shareholder agreement, 75 percent of the net profits after taxes of OLINV would be declared and paid out as a dividend distribution to SSNV. SSNV would in turn declare and pay, pro rata, dividend distributions to its shareholders from the dividends received from OLINV. Accordingly, the fight with the IRS concerned whether the retention of 25 percent of OLINV's after-tax earnings was pursuant to a plan having as one of its principal purposes the avoidance of Federal income taxes.

The Tax Court determined that Dittler was denied a favorable ruling on two grounds. First, the IRS concluded that neither SSNV nor OLINV would devote the property received (manufacturing know-how) to the active conduct of a trade or business, within the meaning of section 3.02(1) of Rev. Proc. 68-23, 1968-1 C.B. 821. Second, the transaction created a potential for tax avoidance in that income from the exploitation of the manufacturing know-how would be diverted to a passive recipient in a benign foreign tax country.

Perhaps the most significant part of the judgment is when the Court stated that:

> Neither Congress in its hearings nor respondent in his rulings has ever defined what is meant by a "principal purpose."

> Although we have never interpreted the term principal purpose within the context of section 367, we have interpreted the meaning of principal purpose in a somewhat analogous provision under section 269. That section, unlike section 367, focuses on whether the principal purpose for which an acquisition was made is the evasion or avoidance of Federal income tax. For section 269 to apply, *principal purpose has been interpreted to mean a tax-evasion or avoidance purpose which outranks or exceeds in importance, any other purpose. VGS Corp. v. Commissioner*, 68 T.C. 563, 595 (1977): *Capri, Inc. v. Commissioner*, 65 T.C. 162, 178 (1975).

> In contrast to section 269, section 367 speaks in terms of a plan having as one of its principal purposes the avoidance of Federal income taxes. When these two statutory provisions are laid side by side, it becomes apparent that *the subjective tax-avoidance motive in section 269 acquisitions must be greater than the tax-avoidance motive in section 367 transfers.* Consequently, section 269 is instructive in the instant case by defining the nature and scope of the tax-avoidance purpose.

> However, because of the statutory variance between section 269 and section 367, with respect to the intendment of the respective statutes, *we believe that the term "principal purpose" should be construed in accordance with its ordinary meaning.* Such a rule of statutory construction has been endorsed by the Supreme Court. *Malat v. Riddell*, 383 U.S. 569, 571 (1966). Webster's New Collegiate Dictionary defines *"principal"* as *"first in rank, authority, importance, or degree."* Thus, *the proper inquiry hereunder is whether the*

exchange of manufacturing know-how was in pursuance of a plan having as one of its "first-in-importance" purposes the avoidance of Federal income taxes.[11] [emphasis added]

In conclusion, the issue centers on the correct meaning on the term "principal purpose". In other words, is a principal purpose standard met only when the avoidance of tax exceeds in importance any other purpose, as stated in *Dittler*? Or is the standard also operative when the tax-avoidance motive was only one of the factors that weighed heavily in the taxpayer's thinking, as argued in *Santa Fe*? Obviously, on the one hand, taxpayers would prefer the former interpretation, which is more lenient, because this allows them to preserve treaty benefits by asserting a relatively weak business purpose; on the other hand, tax authorities would prefer the latter, stricter, interpretation because it permits them to deny treaty benefits if tax avoidance was just more than a trivial or *de minimis* purpose.

Analysis of the legislative history and regulations of section 129 of the 1939 IRC, predecessor to section 269, as well as the extensive case law before and after *Dittler*, clearly suggests that any standard using a principal purpose is met only when the purpose of evading tax exceeds in importance any other purpose.

Therefore, if the US's ultimate goal were to incorporate these new anti-abuse rules in its model treaty and, at the same time, provide certainty to its business community that other countries' tax authorities will not inappropriately invoke the main purpose provisions to challenge legitimate business transactions, why cite the ambiguous *Santa Fe* ruling? In my opinion, the US should have requested the inclusion of an additional provision in the Protocol to the tax treaty with Italy, clarifying the scope of the "main purpose" provision, which reads as follows: "As was discussed and understood among the negotiators, the following Articles 10(10); 11(9); 12(8) and 22(3) should be operative only if the tax evasion or avoidance purpose outranks or exceeds in importance, any other purpose."

The rejection of main purpose tests in the tax treaties with Italy and Slovenia based on the incorrect interpretation of the term given in *Santa Fe* could be considered a posteriori to have been a strategic mistake. Oddly, in 1999, the US did not take advantage of the opportunity

---

11 *Dittler Brothers, Inc. v. Commissioner of Internal Revenue*, USTC, 27 Aug. 1979, 72 T.C. 896, 914–15, 17 (emphasis added).

to play a leadership role in shaping the future direction of this important principle. The fact that the PPT rule is currently included in more than 1,100 matched agreements demonstrates how important it was to the US in 1999 to adopt such a standard in the tax treaties with Italy and Slovenia. However, as mentioned, the inclusion of this standard should have been explicitly based on the *Dittler* ruling, the only approach able to ensure a consistent and reasonable application of the standard. In 1999, the US lost the chance to unilaterally impose its own interpretation of the PPT rule. Today, with the US refusing to sign up to the MLI, the concerns of Ms Paull and of Senator Hagel as to whether other countries' tax authorities would appropriately administer this provision are more important than ever.

12.6   Anti-hybrid provisions

Similarly to the ATAD, TRA17 contains two anti-hybrid provisions that directly implement the single tax principle. The first, section 14101 of the Senate amendment, the new section 245A(e), disallows the participation exemption for hybrid dividends that are treated as deductible payments at source. The second, section 14223 of the Senate amendment, the new section 267A, limits the deductibility of payments on hybrid instruments or to hybrid entities. These provisions clearly implement OECD BEPS Action 2 in accordance with the single tax principle.

In particular, on the one hand, section 245A(e)(1) provides that the dividend received deduction is not available for any dividend received by a US shareholder from a CFC if the dividend is a "hybrid dividend". Hybrid dividend is defined as "an amount received from a controlled foreign corporation for which a deduction would be allowed under this provision and for which the specified 10-percent owned foreign corporation received a deduction (or other tax benefit) from taxes imposed by a foreign country". In addition, if a CFC receives a hybrid dividend from another CFC, the hybrid dividend is treated as Subpart F income. Finally, section 245A(e)(3) provides, by reference to section 245A(d)(1) and (2), that no foreign tax credit or deduction is allowed for any taxes paid or accrued with respect to a hybrid dividend.

On the other hand, section 267A(a) denies a deduction for any "disqualified related party amount" paid or accrued pursuant to a "hybrid transaction" or by, or to, a "hybrid entity". A disqualified related party amount is any interest or royalty paid or accrued to a related party to the extent that: (a) there is no corresponding inclusion to the related party under the tax law of the country of which such related party is a resident for tax purposes or is subject to tax, or (b) such related party is allowed a deduction with respect to such amount under the tax law of such country. A hybrid transaction is defined as

> any transaction, series of transactions, agreement, or instrument one or more payments with respect to which are treated as interest or royalties for Federal income tax purposes and which are not so treated for purposes of the tax law of the foreign country of which the recipient of such payment is resident for tax purposes or is subject to tax.

Finally, a hybrid entity is any entity which is either: (a) treated as fiscally transparent for Federal income tax purposes but not so treated for purposes of the tax law of the foreign country of which the entity is resident for tax purposes or is subject to tax, or (b) treated as fiscally transparent for purposes of the tax law of the foreign country of which the entity is resident for tax purposes or is subject to tax but not so treated for Federal income tax purposes.

It may seem strange that the US took this action while making the CFC-to-CFC look-through rule section 954(c)(6) permanent and thereby facilitating foreign-to-foreign profit shifting from high- to low-tax jurisdictions abroad. The fundamental question is whether all of this is consistent with the spirit of BEPS. Eventually, the US will tax at residence if there is no tax at source (section 245A(e)) and will tax at source if there is no tax at residence (section 267(a)). But what about the case where both source and residence are foreign? The US will not impose tax and will leave this situation to the foreign jurisdictions to resolve by adopting their own anti-BEPS rules, like the new ATAD II. Again, a strategic mistake made by the US?

Early commentators highlighted how TRA17 prevents the use of hybrid instruments or entities that could reduce the US tax base but does not have any material impact on "foreign-to-foreign hybrid planning, the type of United States multinational planning that many countries blame on the United States check-the-box rule'". In the same vein, a Baker McKenzie Client Alert stated:

> The new provision is a very limited version of the much broader anti-hybrid provisions recommended by the OECD under BEPS Action 2. In particular,

the rules only apply to interest and payments, and only *to outbound payments. There is no equivalent provision that subjects hybrid income paid by a foreign related party to tax in the US where that income would otherwise escape US tax.* Moreover, the definitions of "hybrid entity" and "hybrid transaction" are relatively narrow, so that the new Code Section would not seem to apply, for example, to permanent establishment hybrid mismatches.[12]

Thus, neither section 245A(e) nor section 267A(a) will significantly impact foreign reverse hybrid entities, i.e., entities that are treated as opaque by a foreign investor and transparent under the jurisdiction where they are established, such as a Dutch CV-BV or a Luxembourg SCS-Sarl structure. This might have adverse consequences for both US multinationals and tax authorities, considering that ATAD II also includes specific rules aimed at reverse hybrid mismatches, namely Article 9a.

Over recent years, US multinationals have widely used either a Dutch CV-BV (Starbucks) or a Luxembourg SCS-Sarl structure (Amazon) in order to defer US taxation on their non-US earnings. A US multinational establishes a limited partnership under Dutch (CV) or Luxembourg (SCS) law, which is a fiscally transparent entity under local law but elects to be treated as a corporation for US tax purposes. The CV/SCS licenses international IP rights from the US parent company and further develops such IP under an R&D contract (CRA) or CSA arrangement with the US parent. It then grants an IP licence to a Dutch (BV) or Luxembourg (Sarl) principal. The BV/Sarl may either (a) sell products throughout Europe and retain local in-country service companies for support services, or (b) grant sub-licences to European operating companies. The tax consequences are the following: (a) service or operating companies across Europe remit local country tax on routine income; (b) the BV remits 25 percent tax on net sales or licensing income reduced by royalty payments to the CV; (c) there is no Dutch withholding on royalties under domestic law; (d) the CV is treated as a pass-through for Dutch purposes and thus is not subject to Dutch tax; and (e) the US parent achieves deferral of US tax on its non-US profits as a result of the CV/SCS's hybrid treatment. On the one hand, the US treats the CV/SCS as a corporation and, as a consequence, income that it earns will not generally be subject to current US tax. Moreover, even if the CV/SCS is treated as a CFC, interest and

---

12 Baker McKenzie, *supra* (emphasis added).

royalty income earned from the BV/Sarl, which otherwise would qualify as Subpart F income, may nonetheless not be subject to current US taxation as a result of either section 954(c)(3) or section 954(c)(6). On the other hand, payments to the CV/SCS are also generally not subject to tax in the foreign jurisdiction in which it is established or organized (either the Netherlands or Luxembourg) because the foreign jurisdiction views the CV/SCS as a fiscally transparent entity and therefore treats its income as derived by its owners, including its US owners.

It should be noted that as from January 1, 2020, the benefit of tax deferral for US MNEs derived from setting up those structures in the Netherlands or Luxembourg will probably disappear due to the general hybrid mismatch rules of ATADII, whose territorial scope has been extended to third countries. In particular, Article 9(2)(a) of ATADII states that, "[t]o the extent that a hybrid mismatch results in a deduction without inclusion, the deduction shall be denied in the Member State that is the payer jurisdiction".

This means that where the CV/SCS owns IP and licenses such IP back-to-back through the BV/Sarl in exchange for a royalty payment or enters into loan agreements with the BV/Sarl and/or its subsidiaries to lend surplus cash back to group companies, the payments of interest and royalties by the BV/Sarl to the CV/SCS should no longer be deductible. In those cases, indeed, the interest or royalty deduction will be denied in the payer's jurisdiction, i.e., the Netherlands and Luxembourg.

In addition, as mentioned above, ATADII also provides specific rules aimed at reverse hybrid mismatches. Article 9a(1) states:

> Where one or more associated non-resident entities holding in aggregate a direct or indirect interest in 50 percent or more of the voting rights, capital interests or rights to a share of profit in a hybrid entity that is incorporated or established in a Member State are located in a jurisdiction or jurisdictions that regard the hybrid entity as a taxable person, the hybrid entity shall be regarded as a resident of that Member State and taxed on its income to the extent that that income is not otherwise taxed under the laws of the Member State or any other jurisdiction.

This specific rule, which takes precedence over the general reverse hybrid mismatch rule of Article 9(2)(a), will become effective as of January 1, 2022. The Netherlands unsuccessfully tried to postpone the effective date to January 1, 2024 "to give third countries, like the United States, sufficient time to amend their legislation to neutralize the effects of a hybrid mismatch in the country of the payment recipient". Indeed, according to the OECD BEPS Action 2 Report (Recommendation 5), mismatch arrangements can also be addressed through changes to domestic law. The residence state of the foreign investor, in this case, the US, could improve its CFC regime in order to ensure that income earned by the CV/SCS will be currently subject to US tax. As will be described below, this could be done by closing the two biggest loopholes of the Subpart F regime, namely the same-country exception of section 954(c)(3) and the look-through exception of section 954(c)(6). However, such proposals should consider whether US MNEs will end up being less competitive than foreign multinationals since they will not be able to redeploy their foreign earnings overseas without an additional US tax burden.

Regardless of the actions that have been undertaken by the US, as a result of Article 9a(1), since the parent company is located in a jurisdiction (the US) that treats the CV/SCS as a corporation, the CV/SCS would be treated as a Dutch or Luxembourg resident entity and taxed on the interest or royalty income received from the BV/Sarl, respectively.

In this regard, the first question that should be asked is whether rules addressing hybrid mismatches are actually necessary. In my opinion, the answer to this is theoretically no, but practically yes. Theoretically no because a textual interpretation of Article 24(4) of the Netherlands-US Income Tax Treaty (1992) suggests that the Netherlands does not have to allow for an exemption from or a reduction of Dutch tax. Article 24(4) of the treaty reads as follows:

> In the case of an item of income, profit or gain derived through a person that is fiscally transparent under the laws of either State, such item shall be considered to be derived by a resident of a State to the extent that the item is treated for the purposes of the taxation law of such State as the income, profit or gain of a resident.

As mentioned above, the CV is viewed as a pass-through entity for Dutch purposes, but as a company for US tax purposes, when it receives interest or dividends from its operating subsidiary, BV. As a result of this hybrid treatment, income earned by the CV generally would not currently be subject to tax in either the US or the Netherlands.

Consequently, Article 24(4) provides that the withholding rate should not be reduced.

This view was initially also confirmed by J.G. Wine, State Secretary for Finance in a letter of May 3, 2005 to the President of the Senate of the States General, where he argued that the Netherlands was no longer obliged to reduce the withholding rate on dividends and interest paid by the BV to the CV. He justified this result based on the purpose of the hybrid entity provision, according to which differences in the qualification of an entity should not lead to situations of double taxation or double non-taxation.

However, in the same letter he also mentioned he was investigating the possibility of granting certain tax benefits to US MNEs that made use of such structure. If real and substantial activities had been performed in or via the Netherlands, Article 24(4) would not have been applied. Therefore, on July 6, 2005, the State Secretary for Finance published Decree IFZ2005/546M, according to which treaty benefits will be granted to an entity that is classified as transparent for Netherlands tax purposes and as non-transparent for US tax purposes, provided that the Netherlands subsidiary carries out real activities. In this regard, a company may request an advance tax ruling confirming that real activities are carried out. The Decree considered the following points as being relevant for the purposes of determining whether real activities are carried out: (a) whether the dividend distributing company is (for tax purposes only) established in the Netherlands; (b) whether directors and/or employees are active in the Netherlands; (c) whether these directors have sufficient professional knowledge; (d) where important decisions are taken; (e) where the company's primary bank account is kept; (f) where the bookkeeping takes place; (g) the amount of equity and debts; (h) which activities are carried out in or through the Netherlands; (i) whether the employees active in the Netherlands are sufficiently qualified; (j) where real risks are run, and (k) whether the remuneration for the activities carried out and the risks run is at arm's length.

Granting treaty benefits to entities that do not qualify based on the literal interpretation of Article 24(4) is the reason I believe that hybrid mismatch rules are necessary in practice. In the absence of any tax holiday granted to foreign direct investors, Article 24(4) is perfectly adequate since it provides that dividend withholding tax should not be reduced. Indeed, similar provisions to Article 24(4) have been included in the treaties with Canada, Denmark, France, Iceland, Ireland, Italy, South Africa, Thailand, and Venezuela. In particular, examples in the Technical Explanation address the issue of reverse hybrid entities. The language contained in the Technical Explanation to Article IV(7)(a) of the Canada–US Income and Capital Tax Treaty (1980) is very clear:

> For example, assume USCo, a company resident in the United States, is a part owner of CanLP, an entity that is considered fiscally transparent for Canadian tax purposes, but is not considered fiscally transparent for U.S. tax purposes. CanLP receives a dividend from a Canadian company in which it owns stock. Under Canadian tax law USCo is viewed as deriving a Canadian-source dividend through CanLP. For U.S. tax purposes, CanLP, and not USCo, is viewed as deriving the dividend. Because the treatment of the dividend under U.S. tax law in this case is not the same as the treatment under U.S. law if USCo derived the dividend directly, subparagraph 7(a) provides that USCo will not be considered as having derived the dividend.

Canada is therefore not obliged to grant treaty benefits, e.g. reduction or elimination of dividend withholding tax imposed under domestic law. Here, the taxable event is the distributive share of dividend paid to CanLP. Because the distributive share of dividend income is not taxed in the US, there is no reduction in Canadian withholding tax on the share belonging to USCo.

The second question that should be asked is, what would be the inter-action between US tax reform and ATADII? In particular, what would be the effect of the new GILTI regime on the CV/BV reverse hybrid structure? Would the hybrid mismatches be shut down? Some practi-tioners have pointed out that since there will be a 10.5 percent immedi-ate tax, it could be argued that the US has resolved the issue of stateless income made possible by the CV/BV structure. In their opinion, due to GILTI, the US no longer allows profits from IP, such as royalty fees, to be transferred out of a Netherlands-based entity without being taxed anywhere. Only time will tell if that is true, but, in that event, EU Member States should refrain from taxing those profits through either the denial of deduction or by including the payments in the taxable income of the reverse hybrid.

In conclusion, it should be noted that all these problems, especially avoiding taxation by other countries of what the US believes is its income, would have been resolved if TRA17 had adopted a similar provision to that proposed by the Obama Administration, according to which sections 954(c)(3) and 954(c)(6) would not have applied to payments made to a foreign reverse hybrid held by one or more US persons when such amounts were treated as deductible payments received from foreign related persons. Indeed, as a consequence of that proposal, the IP income of a CV would currently be subject to US tax. However, the proposal would have modified some of the core provisions of the Subpart F regime, denying the possibility for US MNEs to engage in foreign-to-foreign profit shifting. When the US Congress, on behalf of US multinationals, forced the Treasury to withdraw Notice 98-11, 1998-1 C.B. it used two arguments to justify foreign-to-foreign profit shifting. First, it was said that reduction of foreign taxes through hybrid entities is a good thing for the US Treasury because if US MNEs pay less tax to foreign administrations, that means they will pay more tax to the US when earnings are eventually repatriated. Second, foreign-to-foreign profit shifting is also good economically because US MNEs will have at their disposal more resources that could be used to expand their domestic business operations, thereby increasing the well-being of US workers and customers.

It is therefore clear why TRA17 did not include the Obama Administration's proposal. In my opinion, the US finds itself confronted by a difficult choice: either (a) tax MNEs' offshore income now by eliminating deferral, or (b) do nothing and risk other countries, such as EU Member States through ATAD II, taxing what the US believes is its tax base. Basically, it is like a zero-sum game; if US tax authorities gain, US multinationals lose, and vice versa.

12.7   Conclusion: the future of BEPS

With TRA17, the future of BEPS as the underlying standard of the ITR is assured. As long as the US stood aside, it was not clear that the EU would be able to implement BEPS on its own, and China is only now just beginning to adopt BEPS measures. But TRA17 represents the incorporation of BEPS into US domestic tax law. Moreover, TRA17 should not be considered as a "tax war": it is a long-overdue response to the BEPS by US and other multinationals and a correct application of the single tax principle to prevent double non-taxation. It turns out that the immense effort of the OECD in 2013–15 was not in vain, and a new and better ITR is on the horizon.

13 Full circle? The single tax principle, BEPS, and the new US model

13.1 Introduction: the single tax principle

Since 1997, I have argued[1] that a coherent ITR exists that is embodied in both tax treaties and the domestic laws of most countries, including the US, and that limits the practical ability of countries to adopt any international tax rules they choose. I have further argued[2] that at the core of the ITR are two principles, which I call the benefits principle (active income should be taxed primarily at source and passive income primarily at residence) and the single tax principle (all income should be subject to tax once at the rate derived from the benefits principle, i.e., active income at the consensus corporate rate and passive income at the residence rate for individuals).

This formulation has been highly controversial. While most commentators would agree that the benefits principle has been the core of the ITR since 1923, many deny the validity of the single tax principle and some doubt its coherence. In particular, the single tax principle suggests that whenever the country that has primary jurisdiction under the benefits principle refrains from taxing cross-border income, the other country (residence for active income, source for passive) should tax it instead. This seemed to fly in the face of observed reality because residence countries typically exempt or defer active income, and source countries refrain from taxing many forms of passive income unilaterally without regard to whether it is taxed at residence.

There are, however, elements of US international tax that seem consistent with the single tax principle. The decision in 1918 to prevent double taxation by granting a foreign tax credit rather than an exemption was justified by Thomas Adams in terms of the single tax

---

1 Reuven S. Avi-Yonah, "International Taxation of Electronic Commerce", 52 *Tax L. Rev.* 507 (1997).

2 *Ibid.*

principle. The adoption of the foreign passive holding company rule in 1935, followed by the PFIC rule in 1986, seems intended to ensure effective residence-based taxation of passive income that is unlikely to be taxed at source. The adoption of Subpart F in 1962 was premised on the assumption that the type of income that can be deferred (active income) is likely to be taxed at source at rates comparable to the US rate, and that other types of income (passive and base company income) for which this assumption does not hold should be taxed on a residence basis regardless of the benefits principle (since some of them, especially base company income, are active income that should generally be taxed primarily at source).

These examples all relate to the US as a residence country. As a source country the first US income tax treaty was concluded with France in 1932, and it reduced US withholding taxes (e.g., on royalties to zero) at a time when France was purely territorial, i.e., did not tax foreign source income. Thus, at approximately the same time that the US was enacting the foreign personal holding corporation provisions to ensure that its residents pay tax on income that was unlikely to be taxed at source, it was tolerating double non-taxation of US source income earned by non-residents. The same tolerance applied to US tax treaties, which were commonly extended to tax havens.

This began to change in the 1960s under the guidance of Stanley Surrey, the author of Subpart F and a major architect of the ITR. The first US treaty that indicated that double non-taxation of US source income was inappropriate was the treaty with Luxembourg, which precluded the application of reduced US withholding rates to certain Luxembourgian holding corporations that were not subject to tax on a residence basis. Similar language appears in the 1963 Protocol to the Antilles treaty, in the 1970 US treaty with Finland, and the 1975 US treaty with Iceland. The UK treaty of 1975 imposed limitations on the benefits of corporate residents if the tax imposed by the residence country was "substantially less" than the general corporate tax and 25 percent or more of the company was held by third-country residents. However, the limitation did not apply to UK close companies or to companies held by UK individuals, giving rise to Rosenbloom's comment that "it is difficult to discern a coherent UK treaty policy in the article".[3] The 1978 Protocol to the treaty with France likewise contained only narrow limitations.

---

3 H. David Rosenbloom, "Tax Treaty Abuse: Policies and Issues", 15 *Law & Pol'y Int'l Bus.* 763 (1983).

In general, therefore, US policy before 1979 did not significantly restrict double non-taxation in regard to US source income, despite placing significant unilateral limits on double non-taxation when the US was the country of residence. However, in 1979, following congressional hearings that revealed the extensive use of the Antilles treaty by third-country residents, the US Treasury announced its intention to reexamine the Antilles treaty and a series of treaty extensions to UK colonies and former colonies. In 1981, the US Treasury published the new US Model Tax Treaty, which for the first time included a broad LOB provision applicable to both corporations and individuals. This provision provided that the benefits of reduced withholding under the treaty will not apply to nonpublicly-traded corporations residing in the treaty partner, unless over 75 percent of such corporations are owned by individual residents and their income is not paid out to residents of third countries. Additionally, the LOB provided that treaty benefits will not be available to corporations entitled to a significantly lower tax rate in their country of residence.

Subsequent to the 1981 US Model Tax Treaty, the LOB provision became a standard part of all US treaties. It was next included in the treaties with Cyprus (1981), Jamaica (1981), New Zealand (1982), Australia (1982), Denmark (1983), France (1983), and every US treaty since. Indeed, ever since the Senate in 1981 refused to ratify the treaty with Argentina unless it included an LOB, it has been clear that no US treaty will be ratified without an LOB. And in 1986, Congress created a treaty override by adopting a "qualified resident" test (a simple LOB) in the context of the branch profits tax, which made it applicable to all US treaties, including the majority that did not yet have an LOB provision.

Some argue that the creation of the LOB provision had nothing to do with double taxation, but was meant to prevent the United States from having a "treaty with the world" (i.e., allowing any non-resident to achieve treaty benefits without residing in a treaty jurisdiction) by restricting treaty benefits to residents of that state and not allowing the extension of benefits to residents of other states, regardless of whether they were subject to tax at the residence. This, it can be argued, was also the purpose of the termination of the treaties with the Antilles and other tax havens in 1987.

But, this limited view of the purpose of the LOB provision is inconsistent with the last paragraph of the 1981 model LOB, which explicitly makes the reduction of source-based taxation contingent on taxation at residence without regard to the ownership of the recipient of the income. It is also inconsistent with the contemporaneous views held by Rosenbloom who, as International Tax Counsel from 1977 to 1981, was responsible for the inclusion of the LOB provision in the 1981 US Model Tax Treaty and other treaties of that period. In an article published in 1983, Rosenbloom explained the policy behind the LOB provision:

> Many commentators believe that existing international commerce is, to a considerable extent, structured on the assumption that liberal use of treaties will be tolerated ... The fundamental goal of tax treaties is removal of the negative effects of double taxation ... Since treaties are intended to eliminate double taxation, their benefits should flow to persons who, in the absence of the treaty, might be subject to double taxation. These are persons who, while potentially subject to tax in one country on either a source or a personal basis, are also subject to tax in the other country on a personal basis. A principal task of treaty drafters, then, should be to identify those persons in each country who are subject to that country's personal taxing jurisdiction ... It may prove necessary in some cases to adopt special rules to ensure that taxation on a personal basis is not avoided altogether.[4]

While Rosenbloom later mentioned the "treaty with the world" problem and the revenue impact of allowing third-country investors to benefit from a treaty, the principal thrust of these observations is that the US (as a source jurisdiction) should not reduce its withholding tax, unless it has some reasonable assurance that the income will be subject to tax on a residence basis.

By 1981, the single tax principle had become a foundation block of US international tax policy. As Rosenbloom stated,

> One possible course would be for Country X not to enter into a treaty relationship unless it is satisfied that State Y will be likely to impose a full tax on all persons falling within the personal jurisdiction of State Y. In theory, then, at least a single, substantial tax will be collected.[5]

In 1984, the US adopted the dual consolidated loss rule, which (as Rosenbloom acknowledged in his later critique of the single tax

---

4 *Ibid.*
5 *Ibid.*

principle) was the high point of commitment because it incorporated the principle into domestic US law.

However, subsequent developments have led to significant erosion in the US commitment to the single tax principle. This began in 1984 with the adoption of the portfolio interest exemption, which relieves US source interest from taxation at source without regard to whether it was taxed at residence. The portfolio interest exemption has been followed by the rest of the world because no country can afford to tax interest if the largest economy does not do so.

The decline in the US commitment to the single tax principle continued with a series of enactments that created new exceptions to Subpart F: the repeal of section 956A (1994), the banking and insurance exceptions (1997), and the adoption of check the box (1997). The broad use of check the box to change pre-existing international tax rules like Subpart F was unintended, and was followed immediately by Notice 98-11 that represented an attempt to undo the damage, but the genie was out of the bottle: Congress blocked the Notice from going into effect and subsequently enacted section 954(c)(6) to codify the harmful international effect of check the box. The effect of these provisions was to enable US-based multinationals to defer tax on the Subpart F (passive and base company) income of their CFCs without triggering deemed dividends, resulting in a massive $2.1 trillion that are currently "trapped" in CFCs located in low-tax jurisdictions and that cannot be repatriated because of the 35 percent tax on actual dividends.

Nevertheless, despite these unfortunate developments, in other areas the US did maintain its commitment to the single tax principle. This can be seen especially in the treaty context by the insistence on LOB rules, by the conduit financing regulations under Code 7701(l), and by the enactment of anti-arbitrage provisions like Code 894(c). Even outside the treaty context, the IRS challenged a variety of tax arbitrage schemes that result in double non-taxation, like the STARS transactions and other "foreign tax credit generators". And Congress enacted sections 871(m) (to crack down on the use of derivatives to avoid withholding on dividends) and 901(k) and 7701(o)(2) (to address foreign tax credit tax arbitrage transactions, like the Compaq transaction). It can therefore be argued that the fundamental commitment of the US to the single tax principle remained unchanged despite the portfolio interest exemption and check the box.

The financial crisis of 2008 and the UBS scandal led to increased US concern about both tax evasion (US citizens pretending to be foreigners and abusing the portfolio interest exemption) and tax avoidance (the increased attention to what Ed Kleinbard has dubbed "stateless income" and the realization that BEPS does not just harm other countries but the US as well). The result has been an increased commitment to the single tax principle in both the US and overseas. This can be seen in FATCA and its progeny, in the G20/OECD BEPS project, and in the new US model treaty.

13.2   FATCA and MAATM

FATCA was initially adopted in 2010 in response to the UBS case, and on the face of it FATCA is just about requiring foreign financial institutions to report accounts controlled by US citizens or residents directly to the IRS. Because FATCA has real teeth (non-complying foreign financial institutions (FFIs) that derive US source income are subject to 30 percent withholding) and because it violates local privacy laws, it initially met with huge resistance. But the US Treasury was able to negotiate intergovernmental agreements with over a hundred countries to permit FFIs to transfer the information to their own governments, which would then share it under treaties. That, in turn, led to the development of standard information exchange rules that culminated in the MAATM, which has now been signed by over 80 countries (including the US) and which provides for automatic exchange of information with no bank secrecy or dual criminality exceptions. At the same time, the US has now finalized regulations first proposed in 2000 to require US financial institutions to collect data on payments that qualify for the portfolio interest exemption.

These developments promise to deal a significant blow to tax evasion and consequent double non-taxation. In fact, Gabriel Zucman has recently estimated that total global tax evasion is only $200 billion annually, which may seem like a big number but is actually very small in comparison to overall financial income. His estimate of US tax evasion and avoidance is only $36 billion, which is much smaller than some previous estimates (e.g., a commonly used number of $100 billion which conflates tax evasion and avoidance, or my 2005 estimate of $50 billion for tax evasion). It may be that Zucman is underestimating, but it is also possible that the deterrence effect of FATCA and

MAATM has worked and that the scope of the problem is indeed smaller now than it was before 2010.

In any case, these developments indicate a global commitment to enforce taxation of passive income at residence and to limit the scope of the portfolio interest exemption by subjecting payments to potential automatic exchange of information. It should be remembered that even the original portfolio interest exemption has a provision (Code 871(h)(6)) that authorizes the Treasury to suspend the exemption for countries that do not cooperate with exchange of information. This provision has much more bite in the age of MAATM.

13.3   BEPS

In introducing the final BEPS package on October 5, 2015, OECD Secretary-General Angel Gurria stated:

> Base erosion and profit shifting affects all countries, not only economically, but also as a matter of trust. BEPS is depriving countries of precious resources to jump-start growth, tackle the effects of the global economic crisis and create more and better opportunities for all. But beyond this, BEPS has been also eroding the trust of citizens in the fairness of tax systems worldwide. The measures we are presenting today represent the most fundamental changes to international tax rules in almost a century: they will put an end to double non-taxation, facilitate a better alignment of taxation with economic activity and value creation, and when fully implemented, these measures will render BEPS-inspired tax planning structures ineffective.[6]

While this is no doubt over-optimistic, there is no questioning the new resolve of the G20 and OECD to uphold the single tax principle. This goal can be seen in all of the BEPS Action steps.

13.3.1   BEPS Action steps

Action 1: Addressing the tax challenges of the digital economy

This step is designed to address the ability of multinationals to avoid taxation of active income at source by selling goods and services into an economy without having a PE. In a world in which most residence

---

6   OECD press release, October 5, 2015 (emphasis added).

jurisdictions exempt or defer taxation of active income, changing the PE physical presence standard is essential to prevent double non-taxation.

Action 2: Neutralising the effects of hybrid mismatch arrangements

This step is obviously designed to address double non-taxation by limiting tax arbitrage transactions designed to utilize hybrid mismatches to create double non-taxation. Check the box is a target.

Action 3: Designing effective controlled foreign company rules

This step is intended to enforce effective residence-based taxation of income that is not taxed at source by limiting the scope of exemption and deferral to income that is subject to source-based taxation.

Action 4: Limiting base erosion involving interest deductions and other financial payments

This step is designed to enforce source-based taxation of active income by limiting interest and related deductions that erode the corporate tax base without corresponding inclusions at residence.

Action 5: Countering harmful tax practices more effectively, taking into account transparency and substance

This step is intended to reinforce source-based taxation of active income by putting limits on harmful tax competition involving special regimes like patent boxes and cashboxes, and by requiring real investment that raises the transaction costs.

Action 6: Preventing the granting of treaty benefits in inappropriate circumstances

This action adopts the US LOB position that treaty benefits should not result in reduction of tax at source unless there is effective taxation at residence, including a "main purpose test" that states that the purpose of treaties is to prevent both double taxation and double non-taxation. The new preamble to the OECD model states that "[State A] and [State B] ... Intending to conclude a Convention for the elimination of double taxation with respect to taxes on income and on capital *without creating opportunities for non-taxation or reduced taxation through tax evasion or avoidance*" [emphasis added].

Action 7: Preventing the artificial avoidance of permanent establishment status

This action reinforces source-based taxation of active income and prevents the shifting of such income into low-tax jurisdictions through commissionaire and similar arrangements.

Actions 8–10: Aligning transfer pricing outcomes with value creation

These actions build on earlier OECD work by limiting the ability to shift income to low-tax jurisdictions by transfer pricing.

Action 11: Measuring and monitoring BEPS

This action attempts to incentivize governments to act on BEPS by measuring its magnitude (between $100 and $240 billion reach year in tax avoided).

Action 12: Mandatory disclosure rules

This action seeks to prevent secret rulings that enable multinationals to pay very low effective tax rates in countries that appear to have high corporate tax rates.

Action 13: Guidance on transfer pricing documentation and country-by-country reporting

This action seems to bolster transfer pricing by requiring CbCR by multinationals, so that tax avoidance can be measured and source taxation of active income upheld.

Action 14: Making dispute resolution mechanisms more effective

This action builds on previous OECD work on mandatory arbitration in tax treaties to prevent double taxation. It is a necessary corollary to the steps that limit double non-taxation.

Action 15: Developing a multilateral instrument to modify bilateral tax treaties

This action is intended to improve coordination of the previous steps.

13.3.2 Conclusion

Overall this is a very impressive achievement in a very short span of time. While BEPS will not eliminate double non-taxation any time soon, it demonstrates significant political commitment by the G20 and OECD to the single tax principle. It builds on earlier OECD actions like the commentary on Article 1 that incorporates LOB principles, and that according to OECD applies to all treaties that include Article 1, which is every tax treaty.

Whatever we think about the efficacy of BEPS (and I have some doubts in this regard and in regard to the actual outcomes incorporated in the final package, which inevitably reflect political compromises as well as MNE push-back), I think the OECD CTPA did an amazing job in a very short timeframe. BEPS represents a greater commitment to the single tax principle than anything that has happened since 1927, and that by itself is a major achievement.

13.4 The new US model

Anticipating the outcome of BEPS, the US in May 2015 released several proposed amendments to its model tax treaty, all of which are consistent with the single tax principle.

13.4.1 Treaty-exempt PEs

New Article 1 section 7 excludes from the withholding tax reductions of the treaty payments to a PE of a company of the treaty partner in a third state if:

> the profits of that permanent establishment are subject to a combined aggregate effective rate of tax in the [treaty partner state] and the state in which the permanent establishment is situated of less than 60 percent of the general rate of company tax applicable in the [treaty partner state]

or if the PE is situated in a third state that does not have a tax treaty with the US and the PE is not subject to tax in the treaty partner.

This provision is intended to prevent treaty benefits accruing to a company resident in a treaty party that applies territoriality so as to exclude the profits of branches in low-tax jurisdiction. The effect of the provision would be to impose full 30 percent withholding on payments to such branches, consistently with the single tax principle and the branch rule of Subpart F.

13.4.2   Expanded LOB

The new LOB article is a significant tightening of existing LOB rules. For example, the requirement that if a company is traded on a stock exchange, that stock exchange must be in the same country that the company is in, is intended to address "inversion" transactions in which US companies inverted to Bermuda, had the board meet in Barbados to qualify under the US–Barbados treaty, and claimed exemption from LOB because they were publicly traded on the New York Stock Exchange.

In addition, similarly to the 1981 LOB, treaty benefits are denied to a company unless:

> ii) with respect to benefits under this Convention other than under Article 10 (Dividends), less than 50 percent of the company's gross income, and less than 50 percent of the tested group's gross income, is paid or accrued, directly or indirectly, in the form of payments that are deductible for purposes of the taxes covered by this Convention in the company's Contracting State of residence (but not including arm's length payments in the ordinary course of business for services or tangible property), either to persons that are not residents of either Contracting State entitled to the benefits of this Convention under subparagraph (a), (b), (c) or (e) of this paragraph *or to persons that meet this requirement but that benefit from a special tax regime in their Contracting State of residence with respect to the deductible payment.* [emphasis added]

"Special tax regime" is a newly defined term:

> l) the term "special tax regime" with respect to an item of income or profit means any legislation, regulation or administrative practice that provides a *preferential effective rate of taxation* to such income or profit, *including through reductions in the tax rate or the tax base.* With regard to interest, the term special tax regime includes notional deductions that are allowed with respect to equity. However, the term shall not include any legislation, regulation or administrative practice:
>
> i) the application of which does not disproportionately benefit interest, royalties or other income, or any combination thereof;

ii) that, with regard to royalties, satisfies a substantial activity requirement;

iii) that implements the principles of Article 7 (Business Profits) or Article 9 (Associated Enterprises);

iv) that applies principally to persons that exclusively promote religious, charitable, scientific, artistic, cultural or educational activities;

v) that applies principally to persons substantially all of the activity of which is to provide or administer pension or retirement benefits;

vi) that facilitates investment in entities that are marketed primarily to retail investors, are widely-held, that hold real property (immovable property), a diversified portfolio of securities, or any combination thereof, and that are subject to investor-protection regulation in the Contracting State in which the investment entity is established; or

vii) that the Contracting States have agreed shall not constitute a special tax regime because it does not result in a low effective rate of taxation. [emphasis added]

This means that the withholding tax reductions of the treaty will not apply to a company if 50 percent or more of its income (or of the income of its consolidated group) is paid in deductible payments either to residents of third countries or to a company in the treaty partner country that is subject to a low effective tax rate because of a "special tax regime". As in the 1981 LOB, this provision makes it clear that the purpose of the LOB is to enforce the single tax principle, not just to prevent a treaty with the world.

13.4.3   Anti-inversion rules

New language is added to Articles 10, 11, 12, and 21 to the effect that dividends, interest, royalties, and other income paid by an "expatriated entity" can be subject to 30 percent withholding tax for a period of ten years after the inversion that created it. Since most "second wave" inversions are to treaty jurisdictions and the treaty is essential to the purpose of the inversion, which is to generate double non-taxation by stripping earnings out of the US into low-tax jurisdictions (e.g., through the Netherlands or Ireland, as in the infamous Double Irish Dutch Sandwich), this will be a significant blow to inversions when it is included in actual treaties.

13.4.4   Special tax regimes

The newly defined "special tax regime" will, in accordance with the Technical Explanation, also prevent reduction of withholding taxes under Articles 11, 12, and 21.

The Technical Explanation provides that:

> Subparagraph 1(l) defines the term "special tax regime" with respect to an item of income. The term is used in Articles 11 (Interest), 12 (Royalties), and 21 (Other Income), each of which denies treaty benefits to items of income if the resident of the other Contracting State (the residence State) beneficially owning the interest, royalties, or other income, is related to the payor of such income, and benefits from a special tax regime in its residence State with respect to the particular category of income. This rule allows the Contracting State in which the item of income arises to retain its right to tax the income under its domestic law if the resident benefits from a regime in the residence State with respect to a category of income that includes the item of income that results in low or no taxation. The term "special tax regime" also is used in Article 22 (Limitation on Benefits) for the purposes of the so-called "derivative benefits" rule in paragraph 4 of that Article.
>
> The application of the term "special tax regime" in Articles 11, 12 and 21 is consistent with the tax policy considerations that are relevant to the decision to enter into a tax treaty, or to amend an existing tax treaty, as articulated by the Commentary to the OECD Model, as amended by the Base Erosion and Profits Shifting initiative. In particular, paragraph 15.2 of the introduction of the OECD Model now provides:
>
> > Since a main objective of tax treaties is the avoidance of double taxation in order to reduce tax obstacles to cross-border services, trade and investment, the existence of risks of double taxation resulting from the interaction of the tax systems of the two States involved will be the primary tax policy concern. Such risks of double taxation will generally be more important where there is a significant level of existing or projected cross-border trade and investment between two States. Most of the provisions of tax treaties seek to alleviate double taxation by allocating taxing rights between two States and it is assumed that where a State accepts treaty provisions that restrict its right to tax elements of income, it generally does so on the understanding that these elements of income are taxable in the other State. Where a State levies no or low income taxes, other States should consider whether there are risks of double taxation that would justify, by themselves, a tax treaty. States should also consider

whether there are elements of another State's tax system that could increase the risk of non-taxation, which may include tax advantages that are ring-fenced from the domestic economy.

The term "special tax regime" means any legislation, regulation, or administrative practice that provides a preferential effective rate of taxation to interest, royalties or other income, including through reductions in the tax rate or tax base. In the case of interest, the term includes any legislation, regulation, or administrative practice, whether or not generally available, that provides notional deductions with respect to equity. For purposes of this definition, an administrative practice includes a ruling practice.

For example, if a taxpayer obtains a ruling providing that its foreign source interest income will be subject to a low rate of taxation in the residence State, and that rate is lower than the rate that generally would apply to foreign source interest income received by residents of that State, the administrative practice under which the ruling is obtained is a special tax regime. Paragraph 2 of the Protocol provides a list of the legislation, regulations, and administrative practices existing in the other Contracting State at the time of the signature of the Convention that the Contracting States agree are "special tax regimes" within the meaning of paragraph 1(l) of Article 3.

This is clearly consistent with the single tax principle and with the original US LOB of 1981, which has been eroded in subsequent versions but is now returning with full force to deny treaty benefits (reductions in source taxation) in cases that the effective tax rate at residence is too low.

13.4.5   Subsequent changes

A new Article 28 provides that:

1. If at any time after the signing of this Convention, the general rate of company tax applicable in either Contracting State falls below 15 percent with respect to substantially all of the income of resident companies, or either Contracting State provides an exemption from taxation to resident companies for substantially all foreign source income (including interest and royalties), the provisions of Articles 10 (Dividends), 11 (Interest), 12 (Royalties) and 21 (Other Income) may cease to have effect pursuant to paragraph 4 of this Article for payments to companies resident in both Contracting States.

2. If at any time after the signing of this Convention, the highest marginal rate of individual tax applicable in either Contracting State falls below 15

percent with respect to substantially all income of resident individuals, or either Contracting State provides an exemption from taxation to resident individuals for substantially all foreign source income (including interest and royalties), the provisions of Articles 10, 11, 12 and 21 may cease to have effect pursuant to paragraph 4 of this Article for payments to individuals resident in either Contracting State.

3. For purposes of this Article:

a) the allowance of generally available deductions based on a percentage of what otherwise would be taxable income, or other similar mechanisms to achieve a reduction in the overall rate of tax, shall be taken into account for purposes of determining the general rate of company tax or the highest marginal rate of individual tax, as appropriate; and

b) a tax that applies to a company only upon a distribution by such company, or that applies to shareholders, shall not be taken into account in determining the general rate of company tax.

4. If the provisions of either paragraph 1 or paragraph 2 of this Article are satisfied by changes in law in one of the Contracting States, the other Contracting State may notify the first-mentioned Contracting State through diplomatic channels that it will cease to apply the provisions of Articles 10, 11, 12 and 21. In such case, the provisions of such Articles shall cease to have effect in both Contracting States with respect to payments to resident individuals or companies, as appropriate, six months after the date of such written notification, and the Contracting States shall consult with a view to concluding amendments to this Convention to restore an appropriate allocation of taxing rights.

The Technical Explanation provides that:

The negotiation of the Convention took into account the desire of the two Contracting States to allocate taxing rights between them in a manner that would alleviate double taxation that could otherwise result if cross-border income, profit or gain were taxed under the domestic laws of the two Contracting States. The Contracting States recognize that certain subsequent changes to the domestic laws of one or both of the Contracting States that lower taxation could reduce the risk of double taxation but in addition increase the risk that the Convention would give rise to unwanted instances of low or no taxation. In addition, such subsequent changes in law could draw into question the continued appropriateness of the allocation of taxing rights that was originally negotiated in the Convention.

Article 28 addresses this possibility by providing that if, at any time after the signing of the Convention, either Contracting State enacts certain changes to domestic law that could implicate the terms of the Convention, certain benefits of the Convention may cease to have effect, and if so the Contracting States shall consult with a view to amending the Convention in a way that would restore an appropriate allocation of taxing rights.

Article 28 is consistent with the tax policy considerations that are relevant to the decision to enter into a tax treaty, or to amend an existing tax treaty, as articulated by the Commentary to the OECD Model, as amended by the Base Erosion and Profits Shifting initiative.

Once again the consistency of this provision with the single tax principle is explicit. The goal is to address subsequent harmful tax competition provisions that erode residence-based taxation in the treaty partner.

Overall these provisions show that in the BEPS context the US delegation pushed consistently for the implementation of the single tax principle, while resisting efforts to upset the existing balance between residence and source countries by adopting more radical changes such as formulary apportionment (although CbCR may lead in this direction; this provision was not favored by the US).

13.5   Conclusion

The first model treaty, drafted by the League of Nations Committee of Technical Experts in 1927, explicitly acknowledged the single tax principle in its commentary. The commentary states:

> From the very outset, [the drafters of the model convention] realized the necessity of dealing with the questions of tax evasion and double taxation in co-ordination with each other. It is highly desirable that States should come to an agreement with a view to ensuring that a taxpayer shall not be taxed on the same income by a number of different countries, and it seems equally desirable that such international cooperation should prevent certain incomes from escaping taxation altogether. *The most elementary and undisputed principles of fiscal justice, therefore, required that the experts should devise a scheme whereby all incomes would be taxed once and only once.*[7]

---

7   Report prepared by the Committee of Experts on Double Taxation and Tax Evasion (League of Nations Publications, 1927), 23 (emphasis added).

This language was implemented, for example, in the interest article by providing for a provisional withholding tax that would be refunded upon showing that the interest was declared in the country of residence.

We have now come full circle, in that the US, the OECD and the G20 clearly have adopted the single tax principle as their goal. The specific measures in the final BEPS package fall short of this goal, and the US model treaty provisions have not been incorporated into any treaty. But there is light at the end of the tunnel. With further political pressure, double non-taxation may in fact be on its way to extinction, as Secretary-General Gurria has said. The vision of Adams and Surrey (the principal US architects of the ITR) is closer to fruition now than at any time since the foreign tax credit was enacted in 1918. The US should not let temporary pressures in the opposite direction, like the current legislative push for a patent box or for territoriality, stand in the way.

14 A global treaty override? The new OECD multilateral tax instrument and its limits

14.1 Introduction

On June 7, 2017, 68 countries met in Paris for the official signing ceremony for a new multilateral tax instrument (MLI). The text and commentary of the MLI were published in November 2016 by the OECD, which stated:

> The Multilateral Convention to Implement Tax Treaty Related Measures to Prevent BEPS will implement minimum standards to counter treaty abuse and to improve dispute resolution mechanisms while providing flexibility to accommodate specific tax treaty policies. It will also allow governments to strengthen their tax treaties with other tax treaty measures developed in the OECD/G20 BEPS Project ...
>
> The new instrument will transpose results from the OECD/G20 Base Erosion and Profit Shifting Project (BEPS) into more than 2000 tax treaties worldwide. A signing ceremony will be held in June 2017 in Paris.

The OECD went on to explain that:

> The multilateral convention was developed over the past year, via negotiations involving more than 100 jurisdictions including OECD member countries, G20 countries and other developed and developing countries, under a mandate delivered by G20 Finance Ministers and Central Bank Governors at their February 2015 meeting ...
>
> The OECD will be the depositary of the multilateral instrument and will support governments in the process of its signature, ratification and implementation. A first high-level signing ceremony will take place in the week beginning 5 June 2017, with the expected participation of a significant group of countries during the annual OECD Ministerial Council meeting, which brings together ministers from OECD and partner countries to discuss issues of global relevance.

There is no question that this event represents a milestone in the evolution of the ITR. But it also raises important questions about the function of tax treaties in the twenty-first century, and whether other steps can be taken to improve the tax treaty network beyond the MLI.

To appreciate the importance of the MLI, it is useful to take a step back and consider its historical significance. Bilateral tax treaties were first negotiated in the nineteenth century, but their importance grew after World War I because of increased income tax rates and the risk of double (residence/source) taxation. The result was the publication of the first model bilateral tax treaty under the auspices of the League of Nations in 1928, followed by the Mexico (1943) and London (1946) models. The OECD took over from the League after World War II and published its own bilateral model (based on the London model) in 1963, while the UN published a bilateral model based on the Mexico model in 1980. These models in turn inspired a network of over 2,500 bilateral tax treaties that form the bulwark of the ITR. About 80 percent of the words of any two tax treaties are identical and stem from the OECD or UN models (which are themselves over 80 percent identical with each other).

From the beginning, the League of Nations was interested in the possibility of negotiating a multilateral tax treaty, but concluded that the differences among the tax law of different states are too vast to allow for a successful negotiation. Subsequent efforts to negotiate multilateral tax treaties also failed. Most recently, the European Court of Justice refused to apply its freedom of movement of capital jurisprudence to force a harmonization of withholding tax rates among treaties within the EU.

However, in the academic world as well as in practice, there has been increasing recognition of the need for a multilateral tax treaty. There are three reasons why a multilateral tax treaty makes more sense than a network of bilateral tax treaties. First, the rise of the General Agreement on Tariffs and Trade (GATT) and then the WTO after World War II showed that multilateral treaties governing important areas of international economic law are feasible if space is allowed for reservations (i.e., allowing countries to opt out of specific provisions). Second, there has been increasing convergence in the language of the various tax treaties, and especially the OECD and UN models have become more similar to each other over time. Third, with globalization, tax competition treaty shopping (using treaties to obtain advantages for non-treaty country residents) and "triangular situations" (problems arising from treaty residents doing business in third countries in ways that affect the treaty but are not covered by it) have become far more common.

In addition, the main obstacle to a multilateral tax treaty has always been that investment flows vary by each pair of countries and therefore appropriate withholding tax rates vary as well. That is the main reason for the remaining differences between the OECD and UN models, because flows between developed countries are more reciprocal than flows between developed and developing countries. But even that situation is changing, as more developing countries become capital exporters as well as importers. In addition, it has been recognized for a while that it may be possible to negotiate a multilateral treaty but leave the withholding tax rates to be settled by bilateral negotiation, as the UN model does.

The new OECD MLI represents the culmination of this line of thinking. It is not a full-fledged multilateral tax convention covering all the areas that are usually covered by bilateral tax treaties. Instead, it can be thought of as a global consensual treaty override designed to apply the results of BEPS simultaneously to all the tax treaties where the countries involved agree. The MLI is implemented by countries signing and ratifying it according to their usual constitutional norms and then depositing the ratification with the OECD. Upon ratification, the provisions of the MLI apply to override the relevant provisions of all the bilateral treaties of a depositing country, unless there is a reservation (which is not allowed in some cases involving minimum BEPS standards).

In addition, the new OECD MLI includes a wide-ranging dispute resolution mechanism including mandatory arbitration. Mandatory arbitration has recently been introduced into the OECD and US models, but it is still lacking in the UN model and most actual treaties. The effect of including it in the MLI can be to force binding arbitration on all existing treaties, which is likely to prove controversial.

This chapter will proceed as follows. Section 14.2 summarizes the main provisions of the MLI. Section 14.3 discusses the point of tax treaties in the twenty-first century, because it can be argued that they are less necessary under conditions of tax competition. Section 14.4 raises the question of whether tax treaties could be improved short of a full-fledged multilateral tax treaty by inserting a most favored nation (MFN) provision similar to the one found in bilateral investment treaties (BITs). Such an MFN provision operates over time to create a de facto multilateral treaty without actually negotiating one. Section 14.5 concludes.

14.2   The new OECD multilateral instrument (new MLI)

14.2.1   The mission of the MLI

The mission of the MLI is described in the preamble as follows:

> i) to ensure swift, coordinated and consistent implementation of the treaty-related BEPS measures in a multilateral context; ii) to ensure that existing agreements for the avoidance of double taxation on income are interpreted to eliminate double taxation with respect to the taxes covered by those agreements without creating opportunities for non-taxation or reduced taxation through tax evasion or avoidance (including through treaty-shopping arrangements aimed at obtaining reliefs provided in those agreements for the indirect benefit of residents of third jurisdictions); iii) to implement agreed changes in a synchronized and efficient manner across the network of existing agreements for the avoidance of double taxation on income without the need to bilaterally renegotiate each such agreement.

In short, the overall mission or purpose of the MLI is to implement tax treaty-related BEPS measures in a swift, coordinated, and consistent manner across the network of existing tax treaties (Covered Tax Agreements) in a multilateral context without bilateral renegotiation of each such agreement.

Although tax treaties have played an important role in eliminating double taxation and facilitating globalization of liberal investment and trade in the past decades, the loopholes and mismatches in existing treaties are one of the root causes of widespread unregulated BEPS opportunism. As a comprehensive response, BEPS Actions 2, 6, 7, and 14 have developed a series of treaty-related BEPS measures. Action 2 report aims at neutralizing the effects of hybrid mismatch arrangements. Action 6 report aims at preventing the granting of treaty benefits in inappropriate circumstances. Action 7 report aims at preventing the artificial avoidance of PE status. Action 14 report aims at making dispute resolution mechanisms more effective.

Beyond reflecting the BEPS measures in Articles 3 through 26, the MLI further reinforces the single tax principle by recognizing the importance of ensuring that profits are taxed where substantive economic activities generating the profits are carried out and where value is created, and clarifying the position to avoid and eliminate both double taxation and non-taxation or reduced taxation through tax evasion or avoidance.

Multilateral problems demand multilateral solutions. Implementation of the BEPS package will demand updates to model tax conventions, including the OECD Model Tax Convention and the UN Model Tax Convention, as well as to the bilateral tax treaties following those model conventions. Uncoordinated bilateral updates to the treaty network would be burdensome and time-consuming, and would frustrate the implementation of BEPS measures by creating new BEPS opportunities.

To avoid uncoordinated and inconsistent unilateralism or bilateralism, pursuant to Action 15 Report "Developing a Multilateral Instrument to Modify Bilateral Tax Treaties", the MLI is intended to effectively and efficiently modify existing agreements in a multilateral context by creating and maintaining an effective, transparent, and reliable mechanism assisted by the depositary, the Secretary-General of OECD. The MLI is not an amending protocol to a single existing treaty, and would not directly change the text of existing treaties. Instead, the MLI will be applied alongside existing tax treaties, serving as the compass to empower and enable the modification, interpretation, and application of the Covered Tax Agreements for the purpose of effective implementation of the treaty-related BEPS measures and the single tax principle.

The MLI would strengthen global partnership and facilitate the smooth modification of the Covered Tax Agreements. All parties would benefit from active participation either by developing consolidated versions of their Covered Tax Agreements as modified by the MLI, or by agreeing subsequently to different but functionally equivalent modifications to their Covered Tax Agreement. It is not wise for any party to be marginalized and isolated by the far-reaching reform of ITR led by the MLI and the BEPS project as a whole.

The MLI would ensure the coherent and consistent interpretation of the numerous Covered Tax Agreements. Article 31 of the Vienna Convention on the Law of Treaties requires a treaty to be interpreted in good faith in accordance with the ordinary meaning to be given to the terms of the treaty in their context and in the light of its object and purpose. Thus, the purpose of the MLI and the Covered Tax Agreement should be taken into account for the purpose of precisely understanding "the context" in question. To clarify the intent of the parties to ensure that Covered Tax Agreements be interpreted in line with the mission of the MLI especially in controversial circumstances, Article 6(1) requires the Covered Tax Agreements to be modified to include the penultimate paragraph of the preamble text of the MLI.

In addition to benefiting the governments by closing the BEPS loopholes, the MLI is also intended to benefit the MNEs by improving the transparency and predictability of ITR, and effectively minimizing and/ or solving the disputes over the application of Covered Tax Agreements.

14.2.2   The principled flexibilities in the MLI

The MLI is both principled and flexible in response to the idealism and pragmatism of the BEPS package. The treaty-related minimum standards, including the prevention of treaty abuse under Action 6 and the improvement of dispute resolution under Action 14, must be implemented by and through the operation of the MLI in relation to the Covered Tax Agreements. However, the MLI is principled not only because of its dedication to effective implementation of the minimum standards of BEPS measures, but also because of firm adherence to the single tax principle and multilateralism.

To some extent, it is difficult or even impossible to develop a BEPS solution of one size for all. Recognizing that not all the agreed BEPS measures are minimum standards or hard rules, and given that even the minimum standards could be achieved in multiple different ways, the MLI has to be flexible and moderate to enable the parties substantially and creatively to meet the minimum standards and seek best practice pursuant to the purpose and object of the BEPS project. The parties enjoy a variety of flexibility of solutions to implement the MLI by and through free choice of opt in and/or opt out, win–win mutual agreements based on compromise, and invention of more effective methodology and tools in line with the mission and purpose of the MLI and the BEPS package.

First, the MLI only applies to the Covered Tax Agreements that are specifically listed by the contracting jurisdictions to those agreements, although the MLI is intended to cover all existing tax treaties. A party may choose to exclude a specific agreement from the scope of Covered

Tax Agreements, if such agreement has been recently renegotiated to implement the outcomes of the BEPS project, or is currently under renegotiation for the purpose of implementing those outcomes in the renegotiated agreement.

Second, the Parties may use a reservation to opt out of the entirety or parts of substantial provisions not reflecting the minimum standard in the MLI. The reserved provision will not apply as between the reserving party and all other parties to the MLI, and the reserving party is not obligated to modify the Covered Tax Agreements as foreseen by the reserved provision of the MLI.

Third, the Parties may use a reservation to opt out of the entirety or parts of provisions to be applied to a subset of Covered Tax Agreements in order to preserve existing provisions with specific, objectively defined characteristics. Such reservations will apply as between the reserving party and all contracting jurisdictions to the Covered Tax Agreements covered by such reservations.

Fourth, multiple alternatives or optional provisions addressing a particular BEPS issue offered in the MLI will apply only if all contracting jurisdictions to a Covered Tax Agreement affirmatively and expressly choose to apply them. Parities may also feel free to supplement the main provision of the MLI with an additional provision in the Covered Tax Agreement.

Fifth, the MLI provides great flexibility on the provisions relating to a BEPS minimum standard. Where a minimum standard could be satisfied in multiple alternative ways, the contracting jurisdictions may adopt their own favorite approaches or solutions. In case of conflicts or disputes arising from the different approaches between the contracting jurisdictions, the conflicts are expected to be settled amicably by a mutually satisfactory solution consistent with the minimum standard. If a party's Covered Tax Agreements have already satisfied specific minimum standard, this party may opt out of the provision reflecting this minimum standard. To encourage the honest implementation of minimum standards with best efforts, the effectiveness and adequacy of certain Covered Tax Agreement in satisfying the minimum standard would be tested by the Inclusive Framework on BEPS.

Sixth, although Part VI provides for the mandatory binding arbitration, parties enjoy great autonomy and flexibility on the choice of arbitration rules. Part VI applies only between parties that expressly choose to apply it with respect to their Covered Tax Agreements. The parties that choose to apply Part VI may also formulate their own reservations with respect to the scope of cases eligible for arbitration subject to acceptance by the other parties, despite the defined reservations included in Part VI.

Seventh, the MLI encourages the parties to choose the recommended optional provision. Although many optional provisions are not required in order to meet the minimum standards, they are important soft law rules. Thus, it is wise for the parties to introduce these best practices and policy recommendations into the Covered Tax Agreements. For instance, Article 6 encourages parties to include the flowing optional preamble language in their Covered Tax Agreements, "Desiring to further develop their economic relationship and to enhance their co-operation in tax matters". If all parties voluntarily pledge the allegiance to the mission of the MLI, the solidarity of global partnership is expected to be further strengthened by and through more flexible and practical dialogue, negotiation, exchange, and collaboration on the BEPS project.

14.2.3   The macro structure of the MLI

The MLI of 39 Articles could be seen as a dragon, with the preamble as its eyes, Part I as its head, Parts II through VI as its body, and Part VII as its tail. The core value of single tax principle and almost all treaty-related BEPS measures agreed in the BEPS package have been fully reflected in the MLI.

Part I is intended to clarify the scope of the MLI and interpretation of terms. Under Article 1, the MLI modifies all Covered Tax Agreements as defined in Article 2(1)(a). Article 2 interprets four terms and provides the general rules of interpretation of other undefined terms used in the MLI.

Part II addresses the measures on hybrid mismatches covered by the Action 2 Report. Article 3 addresses treaty provision on transparent entities. In addition to addressing dual-resident entities, Article 4 addresses the tie-breaker rule for determining the treaty residence of dual-resident persons other than individuals covered by the Action 6 Report. Article 5 addresses exemption method and credit method.

Part III addresses treaty abuse covered by the Action 6 Report. The Preamble and Article 6 of the MLI clarify that tax treaties are not intended to be used to generate double non-taxation. Article 7(1) and (4) address the rules aimed at arrangements one of the principal purposes of which is to obtain treaty benefits. Article 7(8) through (13) focus on LOB rule. Article 8 focuses on dividend transfer transactions. Article 9 focuses on transactions that circumvent the application of Article 13(4). Article 10 focuses on anti-abuse rule for PEs situated in third states. Article 11 focuses on application of tax treaties to restrict a Contracting State's right to tax its own residents.

Part IV is intended to amend existing tax treaties to counter the artificial avoidance of PE status covered by the Action 7 Report. Article 12 addresses *commissionnaire* arrangements and similar strategies. Article 13 addresses specific activity exemptions. Article 14 addresses the splitting-up of contracts. Article 15 defines the term "a person closely related to an enterprise" frequently used in Part IV.

Part V and Part VI reflect the Action 14 Report on making dispute resolution mechanisms more effective. Part V targets at improving dispute resolution (from Article 16 through Article 17) by clarifying the elements of a minimum standard to ensure the timely, effective, and efficient resolution of treaty-related disputes and best practices.

Part VI (from Article 18 through Article 26) represents a set of cohesive provisions on mandatory binding arbitration of mutual agreement procedure (MAP) cases, in which the competent authorities are unable to reach timely agreement. It contains both substantive content and modalities of its technical application to Covered Tax Agreements. Rules for compatibility with existing provisions are consolidated in Article 26, rather than being scattered in each Article.

Part VII addresses the procedure issues from Article 27 through Article 39, including signature and ratification, acceptance or approval, reservations, notifications, subsequent modifications of covered tax agreements, conference of the parties, interpretation and implementation, amendment, entry into force, entry into effect, entry into effect of Part VI, withdrawal, relation with protocols, and depositary.

To clarify the approach taken in the MLI, the types of provisions of Covered Tax Agreements intended to be covered and the detailed ways for the MLI to affect Covered Tax Agreements, the accompanying text of "Explanatory Statement To The Multilateral Convention To Implement Tax Treaty Related Measures To Prevent Base Erosion And Profit Shifting" was adopted on November 24, 2016. It reflects the consensus of the negotiators with respect to the MLI. It is intended to clarify the operation of the MLI to modify Covered Tax Agreements, but not intended to interpret the underlying BEPS measures, except with respect to Part VI.

14.3   Why are tax treaties necessary?

Before we proceed to evaluate the MLI, it is helpful to raise a more fundamental question: why are tax treaties needed in the twenty-first century?

Traditionally, tax treaties were thought to be needed to prevent classical "juridical" double taxation, in which both the source and the residence jurisdictions taxed the same taxpayer on the same income, one on the basis of source (in rem) jurisdiction and the other on the basis of residence (in personam) jurisdiction. This problem was the reason the League of Nations drafted the first model "convention for the prevention of double taxation" in 1927–28. But as Stanley Surrey pointed out in 1957 and as Tsilly Dagan has emphasized more recently,[1] tax treaties are not needed to prevent double taxation because almost all residence countries grant relief from double taxation by way of credit or exemption unilaterally, without the need for a treaty. Other double taxation situations (dual residence, source/source) are not always resolved even with a tax treaty in place.

In the same article, Dagan also pointed out that the main function of tax treaties is to enforce the "benefits principle", i.e., the compromise reached in the 1920s between the tax claims of residence and source jurisdictions. Under the benefits principle, which is incorporated into every tax treaty, active (business) income should be taxed primarily at source as long as the taxpayer meets the PE threshold, while passive (investment) income should be taxed primarily at residence. Since without a treaty both active and passive income are taxed at source with relief granted by the residence jurisdiction, the main function of the treaty is to shift the taxing right on passive income from source to

---

1 Tsilly Dagan, "The Tax Treaties Myth", *Journal of International Law and Politics*, 32: 939, (2000).

residence by limiting withholding tax rates. Under the OECD model, withholding taxes are limited to 15 percent for dividends, 10 percent for interest and 0 percent for royalties, capital gains and "other income" (e.g., payments on derivatives). That leaves the residence country with the right to tax such payments without granting too much foreign tax credit.

Dagan goes on to argue that this means that tax treaties are helpful among developed countries because the investment flows are reciprocal, but injurious to developing countries. Others (including the developing countries) have rejected this argument because they believe tax treaties are helpful in attracting investment and guaranteeing some measure of tax stability to the investors.

But are tax treaties necessary to enforce the benefits principle? It can be argued that the answer is "no" under conditions of tax competition. Economists have long argued that a "small, open economy" should not tax inbound investment because the tax will either cause the investment to go elsewhere or be shifted to source country taxpayers, who can be taxed directly. This is not entirely convincing because it may be administratively easier for the source country to levy withholding taxes even if the burden is shifted, but the argument that the investment will go elsewhere is generally convincing, especially for interest but increasingly also for dividends, while capital gains cannot usually be taxed by withholding.

Under conditions of tax competition to attract investment, there are two possible scenarios. The first and more common is that the same return can be earned in many places and is therefore subject to tax competition. For interest that is clearly the case, and this is why after the US unilaterally eliminated its withholding on interest in 1984, most countries went along. No tax treaty is needed to reduce withholding on portfolio interest, while "direct" interest among related parties is better policed by transfer pricing and thin capitalization rules.

In the case of dividends, it can perhaps be argued that the investment is more unique, but (a) it is hard to distinguish dividends from interest, especially if derivatives that can be used to convert equity to debt are not taxed at source, and (b) the uniqueness of equity investments is declining as multinationals become more similar to each other under globalization. In addition, dividends are optional and not deductible, so it is not clear what function is achieved by having a withholding tax on dividends and a tax treaty should not be needed to eliminate such taxes.

This leaves royalties, where the tax treaty is the only effective way to reduce withholding tax. But royalties (and rents) represent economic "rents", i.e., unique returns from specific assets, and in that case it is hard to see what is the rationale for reducing the withholding tax because the investor cannot earn them elsewhere. Admittedly, multinationals have become really adept in locating IP in low-tax jurisdictions and using deductible royalties to shift profits there. But that is precisely a good reason why royalties should be subject to full withholding tax rates by source countries (or alternatively not be deductible). Most royalties in any case are paid within multinationals and represent active income that should be taxed at source.

Thus, it can be argued that treaties are not needed to enforce the benefits principle under conditions of tax competition because the income can either be earned somewhere else, in which case the competition will lead to unilateral erosion of the withholding tax, or not, in which case the withholding tax should not be reduced.

But what about the function of tax treaties to attract investment and guarantee tax stability? While the empirical literature does suggest that tax treaties help investment, the same function can be achieved by BITs. BITs have two advantages over tax treaties: they are functionally multilateral because they contain an MFN clause, and they have much stronger dispute resolution mechanisms. If a source country changes its tax rules in a way that really injures investors, they can force it into binding arbitration under the BIT, as the government of India found out recently when it overturned its own Supreme Court to tax Vodafone retroactively.

So can we just dispense with tax treaties? The question may seem too theoretical to be worth pursuing. However, current US tax reform proposals raise the possibility that the whole bilateral tax treaty network will collapse, and perhaps that is no great loss. Countries will either tax at source or not depending on whether the tax competition market allows them to do so, double taxation will be avoided unilaterally, and in those cases in which source countries can tax, the BIT network (which is larger than the tax treaty network) will prevent abuses by the source country.

However, tax treaties in the twenty-first century have another function: they can serve to enforce the other principle underlying the ITR, namely the single tax principle. The single tax principle is the idea that underlies the OECD BEPS project, namely that cross-border income should not be subject to double taxation but also not to double non-taxation. This means that source taxation should generally not be reduced unless residence taxation is in place.

For active income, the single tax principle can be achieved without a treaty because if this income is not taxed at source, residence jurisdictions can tax it under CFC rules without a tax treaty (in fact, tax treaties have been used in some cases to undermine CFC rules). But for passive income, in the absence of a tax treaty network, reduction of withholding taxes are achieved unilaterally by tax competition without any assurance that the income will be taxed at source. The prime culprit is the US portfolio interest exemption from 1984, which has led not just to massive capital flight from developing countries to the "tax haven" US, but also to US residents pretending to be foreign and investing into the US through "incorporated pocketbooks" in the Cayman Islands and friendly Swiss banks. This practice is illegal but hard to prevent in the absence of withholding or information exchange, and the latter can only be achieved by treaty.

For individual taxpayers, the needed exchange of information to enforce residence-based taxation can be achieved by special treaties like bilateral tax information exchange agreements (TIEAs) and the new MAATM. These instruments do not require a full-fledged tax treaty, although in my opinion they are imperfect, and it would be preferable if the US and the EU could agree to reinstate withholding taxes on interest and only reduce them by treaty (so that only residents in countries that tax income and exchange information could benefit from reduced withholding tax rates). Since portfolio interest is always earned in developed countries, the cooperation of tax havens is not needed to achieve this result.

But for corporate taxpayers, the tax treaty network is needed to implement the single tax principle. That can be seen from the experience of countries that allow one of their treaties to be abused by not enforcing limitation on benefit principles, so any taxpayer can come and use the treaty. The result is reduction in source taxes on active income (business profits, royalties, direct dividends) without assurance that the income is taxed at residence.

The whole point of the BEPS project and the MLI is to enforce the single tax principle by ensuring that source taxation will apply in situations where there is no residence taxation because of tax arbitrage or the use of pass-through entities. And that is why in the absence of the MLI treaties could become useless, but with the MLI they are still quite useful.

A US example can be used to illustrate this point. Before 1984, investors into the US used the Netherlands Antilles treaty as a way of deriving interest, dividends, and royalties from US sources at reduced rates. The Antilles treaty was a "treaty with the world," like the Russia–Cyprus or India–Mauritius treaties (although the latter was recently revised). But in 1984 the US unilaterally terminated the Antilles treaty and at the same time started inserting LOB clauses in all its treaties. LOBs are designed to enforce the single tax principle, and they have become an essential and non-negotiable element in US treaty practice and now through the MLI OECD treaty practice as well.

In the absence of treaties with an LOB, it is increasingly likely that corporate taxpayers could derive not just interest but even royalties without paying tax at source or at residence. That is the situation in Europe because of the EU Directives, which override the treaties. The MLI is designed to prevent this type of BEPS by requiring LOBs so that source taxes are not reduced unless there is likely to be tax at residence. That is why treaties are needed in the twenty-first century, and why the MLI is such a useful addition.

14.4   An MFN clause for tax treaties?

Now that the MLI has been adopted by most of the OECD and G20 (excluding the US), what next?

A full-fledged multilateral tax convention remains an unlikely ideal even if the withholding tax rates and method for preventing double taxation are left for bilateral negotiations. But there may be another way to create a de facto multilateral treaty: inserting an MFN clause into tax treaties.

BITs have MFN clauses. The effect has been that innovations in any given BIT tend to spread automatically, and by now the BIT network is a de facto multilateral one, despite the lack of consensus that derailed the attempt to negotiate the multilateral investment agreement in the 1990s.

The obvious difference between tax treaties ad BITs is that tax treaties directly affect revenues and therefore countries may resists MFNs because that will force them to give up revenue if investment flows differ from one treaty partner to another.

But this argument is not entirely convincing. First, investment flows can change under current treaties, and that does not deter countries from entering treaties. They know that treaties can be renegotiated if the change in flows upsets the treaty bargain.

Second, the knowledge that MFN exists can simply be incorporated in treaty negotiations. Suppose the US had MFN in its tax treaties and that it did not wish to reduce its withholding tax rate on portfolio dividends below 15 percent. Knowing that MFN exists would simply ensure that it sticks by this position because it knows that a lower rate will spread to all existing treaties. On the other hand, suppose the US decided that the right rate for direct dividends is zero rather than 5 percent. Having MFN would mean this new negotiating position spreads automatically to all US treaties without requiring opening treaties to renegotiation.

In the case of a country like the US that already has treaties with most of the countries that it wants to have treaties with, and that already reduces most withholding taxes to zero by its existing treaties (the US model has zero for interest, royalties, capital gains, and other income), adopting MFN is unlikely to lead to significant revenue losses and can make it easier to install innovations like the zero tax rate for direct dividends across the US treaty network. It is likely that other OECD member countries are in the same position. Developing countries may be more reluctant, and should be free to avoid the MFN, but for the OECD including the MFN clause tax treaties would seem a logical next step toward the ultimate goal of a full-fledged multilateral tax convention.

14.5   Conclusion: the MLI and the future of the ITR

The MLI is an important innovation in international law. Hitherto, international economic law was built primarily on bilateral treaties (e.g., tax treaties and BITs) or multilateral treaties (the WTO agreements).

The problem is that in some areas, like tax and investment, multilateral treaties proved hard to negotiate, but only a multilateral treaty can be amended simultaneously by all its signatories.

The MLI provides an ingenious solution: a multilateral instrument that automatically amends all the bilateral treaties of its signatories. If the MLI succeeds, it can be a useful model in other areas, such as investment, where a multilateral agreement was not successful, but there is a growing consensus about the need to adjust the terms of BITs to address investor responsibilities and the definition of investment comprehensively.

Whether the MLI will succeed remains to be seen. While ratification by 68 countries (with more to come) is an achievement, the absence of the US is important, and other OECD members have agreed to only a limited set of provisions. On the other hand, the MLI may prove more appealing to developing countries because it enhances source-based taxation and limits treaty shopping.

Even a limited MLI would be a step forward. The current tax reform proposals in the US pose a significant threat to the ITR, because they would sharply reduce the US corporate effective tax rate to attract investment from other jurisdictions. Countries that wish to limit the damage would be wise to accede to the MLI this year and prevent a massive race to the bottom that could ensue if the US becomes (from the perspective of the rest of the world) a giant tax haven.

Select bibliography

2015

Arritola, Claire, *Follow the Money: A Discussion of the Organisation for Economic Co-Operation and Development's Base Erosion and Profit Shifting Project: Has the US Taken Steps to Adopt A Global Solution to This Worldwide Problem?*, 24 U. MIAMI BUS. L. REV. 85 (2015)

Avi-Yonah, Reuven S., *Who Invented the Single Tax Principle?: An Essay on the History of U.S. Treaty Policy*, 59 N.Y.L. SCH. L. REV. 305 (2015)

Ball, Taylor, *International Tax Compliance Agreements and Swiss Bank Privacy Law: A Model Protecting A Principled History*, 48 GEO. WASH. INT'L L. REV. 233 (2015)

Bean, Bruce W., and Abbey L. Wright, *The U.S. Foreign Account Tax Compliance Act: American Legal Imperialism?*, 21 ILSA J. INT'L & COMP. L. 333 (2015)

Blair-Stanek, Andrew, *Intellectual Property Law Solutions to Tax Avoidance*, 62 UCLA L. REV. 2 (2015)

Blum, Cynthia, *Migrants with Retirement Plans: The Challenge of Harmonizing Tax Rules*, 17 FLA. TAX REV. 1 (2015)

Brock, Gillian, *Chapter 12 What Burden Should Fiscal Policy Bear in Fighting Global Injustice?*, 40 IUS GENTIUM 185 (2015)

Burns, Debra Brubaker, *Golden Apple of Discord: International Cost-Sharing Arrangements*, 15 HOUS. BUS. & TAX L. J. 55 (2015)

Calianno, Joseph, and Brandon Boyle, *IRS Adopts 'Not-Willful' Standard For Relief For Certain Missed Filings Under Sections 367(A) And (E)*, 26 J. INT'L TAX'N 37, 2015 WL 3637562 (May 2015)

DeAngelis, Scott, *If You Can't Beat Them, Join Them: The U.S. Solution to the Issue of Corporate Inversions*, 48 VAND. J. TRANSNAT'L L. 1353 (2015)

Denson, Taylor, *Goodbye, Uncle Sam? How the Foreign Account Tax Compliance Act Is Causing a Drastic Increase in the Number of Americans Renouncing Their Citizenship*, 52 HOUS. L. REV. 967 (2015)

Dick, Diane Lourdes, *U.S. Tax Imperialism in Puerto Rico*, 65 AM. U. L. REV. 1 (2015)

Fleming, J. Clifton, Jr., et. al., *Getting Serious About Cross-Border Earnings Stripping: Establishing an Analytical Framework*, 93 N.C. L. REV. 673 (2015)

Garbarino, Carlo, *The Development of the Comparability Analysis by the Court of Justice of the European Union in the Context of Capital Income Taxation*, 21 COLUM. J. EUR. L. 451 (2015)

Grubert, Harry, *Destination-Based Income Taxes: A Mismatch Made in Heaven?*, 69 Tax
L. Rev. 43 (2015)

Hwang, Cathy, *The New Corporate Migration Tax Diversion Through Inversion*, 80
Brook. L. Rev. 807, 807 (2015)

A. Kane, Mitchell, *A Defense of Source Rules in International Taxation*, 32 Yale J. on
Reg. 311 (2015)

Khanjyan, David, *Demanding Corporate Patriotism: A Regulatory Attempt to Curb
International Corporate Inversions and Stop Tax Avoidance Schemes*, 9 J. Bus.
Entrepreneurship & L. 129 (2015)

Marian, Omri, *Home-Country Effects of Corporate Inversions*, 90 Wash. L. Rev. 1
(2015)

Marisam, Jason, *The Internationalization of Agency Actions*, 83 Fordham L. Rev. 1909
(2015)

Mazur, Orly, *Taxing the Cloud*, 103 Cal. L. Rev. 1 (2015)

Mazur, Orly, *Tax Challenges in the Cloud*, 19 J. Internet L. 3 (2015)

Miller, Valeria Camboni, *International Taxation: The Issue of Tax Evasion by
Corporations*, 23 Dig., Nat'l Italian A.B.A.L.J. 74 (2015)

Otávio Ferreira de Almeida, Carlos, *International Tax Cooperation, Taxpayers' Rights
and Bank Secrecy: Brazilian Difficulties to Fit Global Standards*, 21 L. & Bus. Rev.
Am. 217 (2015)

Qureshi, Asif H., *Coherence in the Public International Law of Taxation: Developments
in International Taxation and Trade and Investment Related Taxation*, 10 Asian J.
WTO & Int'l Health L. & Pol'y 193 (2015)

Rosenzweig, Adam R., *Source as a Solution to Residence*, 17 Fla. Tax Rev. 471 (2015)

Rosenzweig, Adam H., *Defining A Country's "Fair Share" of Taxes*, 42 Fla. St. U. L. Rev.
373 (2015)

Sanchirico, Chris William, *As American as Apple Inc.: International Tax and Ownership
Nationality*, 68 Tax L. Rev. 207 (2015)

Shaviro, Daniel, *The Crossroads Versus the Seesaw: Getting A "Fix" on Recent
International Tax Policy Developments*, 69 Tax L. Rev. 1 (2015)

Shay, Stephen E., et. al., *Designing a 21st Century Corporate Tax – an Advance U.S.
Minimum Tax on Foreign Income and Other Measures to Protect the Base*, 17 Fla.
Tax Rev. 669 (2015)

Shen, Wei, and Casey Watters, *Is China Creating A New Business Order? Rationalizing
China's Extraterritorial Attempt to Expand the Veil-Piercing Doctrine*, 35 Nw. J. Int'l
L. & Bus. 469 (2015)

Song, Jane G., *The End of Secret Swiss Accounts?: The Impact of the U.S. Foreign Account
Tax Compliance Act (FACTA) on Switzerland's Status As A Haven for Offshore
Accounts*, 35 Nw. J. Int'l L. & Bus. 687 (2015)

Spencer, David, *Draft Revisions of The U.S. Model Income Tax Treaty (Part 1)*, 26 J. Int'l
Tax'n 31, 2015 WL 5921753 (October 2015)

Spencer, David, *Draft Revisions of The U.S. Model Income Tax Treaty (Part 2)*, 26 J. Int'l
Tax'n 26 (Nov. 2015)

Spencer, David, *The U.N. Tax Committee, Developing Countries, And Civil Society
Organizations (Part 1)*, 26 J. Int'l Tax'n 42, 2015 WL 9943216 (Dec. 2015)

Terveer, Callyn H., *Desperate Times Call for Desperate Measures: The Cost to Multinational Corporations of Implementing FACTA*, 15 Hous. Bus. & Tax L. J. 300 (2015)

2016

Avi-Yonah, Reuven S., *Hanging Together: A Multilateral Approach to Taxing Multinationals*, 5 Mich. Bus. & Entrepreneurial L. Rev. 137 (Spring 2016)

Avi-Yonah, Reuven S., and Haiyan Xu, *Evaluating BEPS: A Reconsideration of the Benefits Principal and Proposal for UN Oversight*, 6 Harv. Bus. L. Rev. 185 (2016)

Bird, Richard M., *Global Taxes And International Taxation: Mirage And Reality (Part 1)*, 27 J. Int'l Tax'n 50, 2016 WL 7116204 (Nov. 2016)

Bogenschneider, Bret N., *A Theory of Small Business Tax Neutrality*, 15 Fla. St. U. Bus. Rev. 33 (2016)

Brauner, Yariv, *Treaties in the Aftermath of BEPS*, 41 Brook. J. Int'l L. 973 (2016)

Cabezas, Montano, *Reasons for Citizenship-Based Taxation?*, 121 Penn St. L. Rev. 101 (2016)

Chaisse, Julien, *Investor-State Arbitration in International Tax Dispute Resolution: A Cut Above Dedicated Tax Dispute Resolution?*, 35 Va. Tax Rev. 149 (2016)

Christians, Allison, *BEPS and the New International Tax Order*, 2016 B.Y.U. L. Rev. 1603 (2016)

Christians, Allison, and Alexander Ezenagu, *Kill-Switches in the U.S. Model Tax Treaty*, 41 Brook. J. Int'l L. 1043 (2016)

Clausing, Kimberly A., *Competitiveness, Tax Base Erosion, and the Essential Dilemma of Corporate Tax Reform*, 2016 B.Y.U. L. Rev. 1649 (2016)

Cockfield, Arthur J., *Big Data and Tax Haven Secrecy*, 18 Fla. Tax Rev. 483 (2016)

Dagan, Tsilly, *Tax Treaties As A Network Product*, 41 Brook. J. Int'l L. 1081 (2016)

Dagan, Tsilly, *The Currency of Taxation*, 84 Fordham L. Rev. 2537 (2016)

Dean, Steven A., and Rebecca M. Kysar, *Introduction: Reconsidering the Tax Treaty*, 41 Brook. J. Int'l L. 967, 967 (2016)

Dey, Shantanu, *Taxation Of Seconded Expatriates In India: Unsettled Jurisprudence*, 27 J. Int'l Tax'n 50, 2016 WL 4611283 (August 2016)

Elkins, David C., *The Merits of Tax Competition in A Globalized Economy*, 91 Ind. L.J. 905 (2016)

Fleming, J. Clifton, Jr., et. al., *Two Cheers for the Foreign Tax Credit, Even in the BEPS Era*, 91 Tul. L. Rev. 1 (2016)

Fleming, J. Clifton, Jr., et. al., *Defending Worldwide Taxation with A Shareholder-Based Definition of Corporate Residence*, 2016 B.Y.U. L. Rev. 1681 (2016)

Greenberg, Rachel J., *Taking a Byte Out of International Tax Evasion: Combating Base Erosion and Profit Shifting*, 19 Chap. L. Rev. 307 (Winter 2016)

Grinberg, Itai, *The New International Tax Diplomacy*, 104 Geo. L.J. 1137 (June 2016)

Hellerstein, Walter, *A Hitchhiker's Guide to the OECD's International VAT/GST Guidelines*, 18 Fla. Tax Rev. 589 (2016)

Kane, Mitchell A., *Location Savings and Segmented Factor Input Markets: In Search of A Tax Treaty Solution*, 41 BROOK. J. INT'L L. 1107 (2016)

Kaye, Tracy A., *Tax Transparency: A Tale of Two Countries*, 39 FORDHAM INT'L L.J. 1153 (2016)

Kirsch, Michael S., *Tax Treaties and the Taxation of Services in the Absence of Physical Presence*, 41 BROOK. J. INT'L L. 1143 (2016)

Kudrle, Robert T., *Tax Havens and the Transparency Wave of International Tax Legalization*, 37 U. PA. J. INT'L L. 1153 (2016)

Kysar, Rebecca M., *Interpreting Tax Treaties*, 101 IOWA L. REV. 1387 (2016)

Levey, Marc, Imke Gerdes, Giuliana Polacco, James Wilson, and Mark Tonkovich, *The Changing Landscape Of Tax Audits In The United States, Canada, And Europe*, 26 J. INT'L TAX'N 28, 2015 WL 9943215, (Jan./Feb. 2016)

Macdonald, J. Ross, *"Time Present and Time Past": U.S. Anti-Treaty Shopping History, Policy and Rules (or, "Well, Stanley, That's Another Nice Mess You've Gotten Us Into")*, 70 TAX LAW 5 (2016)

Marian, Omri, *The Other Eighty Percent: Private Investment Funds, International Tax Avoidance, and Tax-Exempt Investors*, 2016 B.Y.U. L. REV. 1715 (2016)

Marian, Omri, *Unilateral Responses to Tax Treaty Abuse: A Functional Approach*, 41 BROOK. J. INT'L L. 1157 (2016)

Mason, Ruth, *Citizenship Taxation*, 89 S. CAL. L. REV. 169 (2016)

Mazur, Orly, *Transfer Pricing Challenges in the Cloud*, 57 B.C. L. REV. 643, 643 (2016)

Narotzki, Doron, *Tax Treaty Models-Past, Present, and A Suggested Future*, 50 AKRON L. REV. 383, 383 (2016)

Province, Adam G., *Aggressive Foreign Tax Authorities And Military Agreements: Maintaining Tax Exemption In Sofas To Protect Civilian Contractors From Local-Country Tax*, 27 J. INT'L TAX'N 53, 2016 WL 1377692 (March 2016)

Province, Captain Adam G., *Wait, I Owe How Much in Penalties?: U.S. International Tax Considerations for Servicemembers with Foreign Bank Accounts & Foreign Securities*, ARMY LAW 25 (November 2016)

Ring, Diane, *When International Tax Agreements Fail at Home: A U.S. Example*, 41 BROOK. J. INT'L L. 1185 (2016)

Ring, Diane, *Developing Countries in an Age of Transparency and Disclosure*, 2016 B.Y.U. L. Rev. 1767 (2016)

Roin, Julie A., *Inversions, Related Party Expenditures, and Source Taxation: Changing the Paradigm for the Taxation of Foreign and Foreign-Owned Businesses*, B.Y.U. L. Rev. 1837 (2016)

Rosenzweig, Adam H., *"Thinking Outside the (Tax) Treaty" Revisited*, 41 BROOK. J. INT'L L. 1229 (2016)

Saffie, Francisco, *An Alert from the Left: The Endangered Connection Between Taxes and Solidarity at the Local and Global Levels*, 17 GERMAN L.J. 857 (2016)

Shaheen, Fadi, *How Reform-Friendly Are U.S. Tax Treaties?*, 41 BROOK. J. INT'L L. 1243 (2016)

Shaviro, Daniel, *The Two Faces of the Single Tax Principle*, 41 BROOK. J. INT'L L. 1293 (2016)

Shay, Stephen E., et. al., *R&D Tax Incentives: Growth Panacea or Budget Trojan Horse?*, 69 Tax L. Rev. 419 (2016)

Shi, Xunjie, *Source Rule Trends For Capital Gains From Stock Sales*, 27 J. Int'l Tax'n 51, 2016 WL 3015039 (April 2016)

Spencer, David, *The U.N. Tax Committee, Developing Countries, And Civil Society Organizations (Part 2)*, 27 J. Int'l Tax'n 44 (January 2016)

Stevenson, Ariel, *Recovering Lost Tax Revenue Through Taxation of Transnational Households*, 34 Berkeley J. Int'l L. 100, 100 (2016)

Tavares, Romero J.S., et. al., *The Intersection of Eu State Aid and U.S. Tax Deferral: A Spectacle of Fireworks, Smoke, and Mirrors*, 19 Fla. Tax Rev. 121 (2016)

Wells, Bret, *The Foreign Tax Credit War*, 2016 B.Y.U. L. Rev. 1895 (2016)

Wells, Bret, *International Tax Reform by Means of Corporate Integration*, 20 Fla. Tax Rev. 70 (2016)

Welty, M. Todd, Mark P. Thomas, Laura L. Gavioli, and Cym H. Lowell, *International Tax Disputes: Elements Of Epochal Evolution* 27 J. Int'l Tax'n 29 (April 2016)

White, Sienna C., *Cost Sharing Agreements & the Arm's Length Standard: A Matter of Statutory Interpretation?*, 19 Fla. Tax Rev. 191 (2016)

2017

Agresta, Robert A., *International Tax Planning As A Business Driver*, 5 Penn St. J.L. & Int'l Aff. 538 (2017)

Alley, Clinton, and Joanne Emery, *Taxation of Cross-Border E-Commerce: Avoidance Of Permanent Establishment And Multilateral Modifications To Tax Treaties*, 28 J. Int'l Tax'n 38, 2017 WL 5624630 (Nov. 2017)

Alley, Clinton, and Joanne Emery, *Taxation Of Cross-Border E-Commerce: Response Of New Zealand And Other OECD Countries To BEPS Action 1*, 28 J. Int'l Tax'n 38, 2017 WL 3977933 (Sept. 2017)

Azam, Rifat, *Ruling the World: Generating International Tax Norms in the Era of Globalization and BEPS*, 50 Suffolk U. L. Rev. 517 (2017)

Bird, Richard M., *Global Taxes And International Taxation: Mirage And Reality (Part 2)*, 28 J. Int'l Tax'n 50, 2017 WL 1436393 (March 2017)

Bogenschneider, Bret N., *5 1/2 Problems with Legal Positivism and Tax Law*, 2017 Pepp. L. Rev. 1 (2017)

Cabezas, Montano, *Migration and Taxation in the Popular Imagination*, 62 St. Louis U. L.J. 103 (2017)

Chisholm, Brendan C., *ICRICT Looking to a Future of Actual Tax Reform: An Organizational Analysis of the Independent Commission for the Reform of International Corporate Taxation*, 85 U. Cin. L. Rev. 231 (2017)

Christians, Allison, *A Global Perspective on Citizenship-Based Taxation*, 38 Mich. J. Int'l L. 193 (2017)

Christians, Allison, *Buying in: Residence and Citizenship by Investment*, 62 St. Louis U. L.J. 51 (2017)

Cockfield, Arthur J., *How Countries Should Share Tax Information*, 50 VAND. J. TRANSNAT'L L. 1091 (Nov. 2017)

Cohen, Jerome A., *Law and China's "Open Policy": A Foreigner Present at the Creation*, 65 AM. J. COMP. L. 729 (2017)

Cui, Wei, *Minimalism About Residence and Source*, 38 MICH. J. INT'L L. 245 (2017)

Dagan, Tsilly, *The Global Market for Tax and Legal Rules*, 21 FLA. TAX REV. 148 (2017)

Davis, Tessa, *The Tax-Immigration Nexus*, 94 DENV. L. REV. 195 (2017)

Dillon, Sara, *Tax Avoidance, Revenue Starvation and the Age of the Multinational Corporation*, 50 INT'L LAW. 275 (2017)

Elkins, David, *The Case Against Income Taxation of Multinational Enterprises*, 36 VA. TAX REV. 143 (2017)

Elkins, David, *The Elusive Definition of Corporate Tax Residence*, 62 ST. LOUIS U. L.J. 219 (2017)

Endean, Jon, *A Payoff to Second Best Pragmatism: Rethinking Entity Classification for Foreign Companies*, 14 N.Y.U. J.L. & BUS. 311 (2017)

Ezenagu, Alexander, *Faltering Blocks in the Arguments Against Unitary Taxation and the Formulary Apportionment Approach to Income Allocation*, 17 ASPER REV. INT'L BUS. & TRADE L. 131 (2017)

Faulhaber, Lillian V., *The Luxembourg Effect: Patent Boxes and the Limits of International Cooperation*, 101 MINN. L. REV. (2017)

Feinschreiber, Robert, and Margaret Kent, *International Tax-Based Cost Accounting Comes Of Age*, 28 J. INT'L TAX'N 00, 2017 WL 1436730 (April 2017)

Field, Heather M., *Offshoring Tax Ethics: The Panama Papers, Seeking Refuge from Tax, and Tax Lawyer Referrals*, 62 ST. LOUIS U. L.J. 35 (2017)

Gutman, Harry L., *The Saga of Unfulfilled Business Income Tax Reform*, 89 TEMP. L. REV. 267 (2017)

Kirsch, Michael S., *Citizens Abroad and Social Cohesion at Home: Refocusing A Cross-Border Tax Policy Debate*, 36 VA. TAX REV. 205 (2017)

Li, Ji, *"Strangers in a Strange Land": Chinese Companies in the American Tax System*, 68 HASTINGS L.J. 503 (2017)

Lincoln, Charles Edward Andrew, IV, *Is Incorporation Really Better Than Central Management and Control for Testing Corporate Residency? An Answer to Corporate Tax Evasion and Inversion*, 43 OHIO N.U. L. REV. 359 (2017)

Gormsen, Liza Lovdahl, *State Aid and Direct Taxation and the Big Eruption Between the U.S. and the E.U.*, 62 ANTITRUST BULLETIN 348 (June 2017)

Herzfeld, Mindy, *The Case Against BEPS: Lessons for Tax Coordination*, 21 FLA. TAX REV. 1 (2017)

Karlin, Michael J.A., *We Will Be Landing Soon: A Multinational Survey Of The Treatment Of Income And Gains Of Individuals Who Change Residence*, 28 J. INT'L TAX'N 29, 2017 WL 1436391 (March 2017)

Kim, Young Ran (Christine), *Considering "Citizenship Taxation": In Defense of FACTA*, 20 FLA. TAX REV. 335 (2017)

Lincoln, Charles, *The Myth of "Separate Enterprises" in International Taxation: Approaches to Attribution of Profits to Permanent Establishments*, 22 TRINITY L. REV. 30 (2017)

Lippert, Tyler H., PhD, JD, *OECD Base Erosion & Profit Shifting: Action Item 6*, 37 Nw. J. INT'L L. & BUS. 539 (2017)

Maine, Jeffrey A., *Multinational Efforts to Limit Intellectual Property Income Shifting: The OECD's Base Erosion and Profit Shifting (BEPS) Project*, 20 SMU SCI. & TECH. L. REV. 259 (2017)

Marian, Omri, *The State Administration of International Tax Avoidance*, 7 HARV. BUS. L. REV. 1 (2017)

Medus, Jean-Louis, *BEPS Proposals To Regulate Digital Business: Some Critical Comments*, 28 J. INT'L TAX'N 34, 2017 WL 3434040 (July 2017)

Mitchell, Andrew D. and Emma Gan, *Policy & Legal Issues Raised by the Proposed U.S. Border Adjustable Tax*, 12 ASIAN J. WTO & INT'L HEALTH L. & POL'Y 289 (2017)

Morotomi, Toru, *Japan's Shift to Territoriality in 2009 and the Recent Corporate Tax Reform: A Japan-United States Comparison of Taxing Income from Multinationals*, 14 PITT. TAX REV. 173 (2017)

Oosterhuis, Paul, *The Need for Second-Best Tax Reform Solutions Commentary on: The Saga of Unfulfilled Business Income Tax Reform by Harry L. Gutman*, 89 TEMP. L. REV. 353 (2017)

Ordower, Henry, *Taxing Others in the Age of Trump: Foreigners (and the Politically Weak) As Tax Subjects*, 62 ST. LOUIS U. L.J. 157 (2017)

Rietiker, Daniel, and Anne-Marie Beliveau, *G.S.B. v. Switzerland (European Court of Human Rights): Data Transfer in Tax Evasion Matters Did Not Violate Human Rights*, 5 SUFFOLK U.L. REV. ONLINE 16 (2017)

Ring, Diane M., *Corporate Migrations and Tax Transparency and Disclosure*, 62 ST. LOUIS U. L.J. 175 (2017)

Rohan, Jan, and Lukás Moravec, *Tax Information Exchange Impact on FDI: Tax Havens Case Study*, 62 ST. LOUIS U. L.J. 193 (2017)

Sheppard, Hale E., *Government Wins Fourth Straight FBAR Penalty Case: Analyzing And The Evolution Of "Willfulness"*, 126 J. TAX'N 110, 2017 WL 972499 (March 2017)

Sheppard, Hale E., *Children With Foreign Accounts: Unexpected Tax, Schedule B, Form 8938, And FBAR Issues*, 28 J. INT'L TAX'N 00, 2017 WL 1436734 (April 2017)

Sheppard, Hale E., *Assessing Tax Liabilities Is One Thing, Collecting Them Abroad Is Another: New Case Shows International Reach Of The IRS*, 127 J. TAX'N 205, 2017 WL 4676708 (Nov 2017)

Sheppard, Hale E., *U.S. Gov't Wins Fourth Straight FBAR Penalty Case: And The Evolution Of "Willfulness" (Part 1)*, 28 J. INT'L TAX'N 34 (August 2017)

Sheppard, Hale E., *U.S. Gov't Wins Fourth Straight FBAR Penalty Case: And The Evolution Of "Willfulness" (Part 2)*, 28 J. INT'L TAX'N 22, 2017 WL 3977932 (2017)

Sloss, David, *California's Climate Diplomacy and Dormant Preemption*, 56 WASHBURN L.J. 507 (2017)

Spencer, David, *BEPS And The Allocation Of Taxing Rights (Part 1)*, 28 J. INT'L TAX'N 36, 2017 WL 1436739, (April 2017)

Spencer, David, *BEPS And The Allocation Of Taxing Rights (Part 2)*, 28 J. INT'L TAX'N 46, 2017 WL 2591903 (May 2017)

Spencer, David, *BEPS And The Allocation Of Taxing Rights (Part 3)*, 28 J. INT'L TAX'N 46, 2017 WL 2610801 (June 2017)

Steines, John P., Jr., *Subsidized Foreign Tax Credits and the Economic Substance Doctrine*, 70 Tax Law 443 (2017)

Trenta, Cristina, *Migrants and Refugees: A EU Perspective on Upholding Human Rights Through Taxation and Public Finance*, 62 St. Louis U. L.J. 1 (2017)

Tokic, Genevieve, *Exploring the Intersection of Trade Policy, Immigration, and Tax Law: A Coordinated Tax Response to the "Push" Factors Driving the Current Wave of Migration to the United States from Central America*, 62 St. Louis U. L.J. 137 (2017)

Walker, Andrew, *Proceed with Caution: D(e)riving A Hybrid Down the Tax Treaty on-Ramp*, 70 Tax Law 749 (2017)

Ward, Robert E., Esq., *Look Before You Leap: When Renouncing U.S. Citizenship May Not Be A Good Idea*, Prac. Tax Law (Summer 2017) 21

Ward, Robert E., *The Common Reporting Standard Comes To Canada*, 127 J. Tax'n 165, 2017 WL 4163339 (October 2017)

Yang, James G.S., Richard A. Lord, and Yoshie Saito, *The Evolution of Economic Nexus in Internet Commerce, State Income, and International Taxation*, 21 J. Internet L. 1 (2017)

2018

Australian Guidance on Foreign Companies' CMAC Test of Residency, 29 J. Int'l Tax'n 04 (Sept. 2018)

August, Casey S., and Jordan D. August, *Application of Section 199A to Domestic Taxpayers Engaged in U.S. and Foreign Business Operations*, 45 WGL-CTAX 03 (Sept./Oct. 2018)

August, Jerald David, *Tax Cuts and Jobs Act of 2017 Introduces Major Reforms to the International Taxation of U.S. Corporations*, 32 No. 2 Prac. Tax Law 43 (Winter 2018)

Avi-Yonah, Reuven S., and Haiyan Xu, *A Global Treaty Override? The New OECD Multilateral Tax Instrument and its Limits*, 39 Mich. J. Int'l L. 155 (Spring 2018)

Callahan, Teresa, *Connecticut Treatment of the Federal Repatriation Transition Tax Under IRC §965*, 28 J. Multistate Tax'n 37 (July 2018)

Carman, Paul D., and Christie R. Galinski, *Classification of Exempt Organizations Under U.S. FATCA, U.K. IGA, and OECD CRS*, 29 J. Int'l Tax'n 38 (Aug. 2018)

Chaisse, Julien, and Xueliang Ji, *"Soft Law" in International Law-Making: How Soft International Taxation Law Is Reshaping International Economic Governance*, 13 Asian J. WTO & Int'l Health L. & Pol'y 463 (2018)

Cockfield, Arthur J., *Shaping International Tax Law and Policy in Challenging Times*, 54 Stan. J. Int'l L. 223 (Summer 2018)

Coffill, Eric J., and Huy N. Le, *Navigating California Water's-Edge Issues: CFCs and Repatriations*, 28 J. Multistate Tax'n 8 (July 2018)

Cui, Wei, *Residence-Based Formulary Apportionment: (In)feasibility and Implications*, 71 Tax L. Rev. 551 (Spring 2018)

Devereux, Michael P., and John Vella, *Gaming Destination-Based Cash Flow Taxes*, 71 Tax L. Rev. 477 (Spring 2018)

Engel, David, *Tennessee Provides Guidance on IRC §965 Repatriation Income for Franchise and Excise Tax Purposes*, J. MULTISTATE TAX'N 39 (July 2018)

Faulhaber, Lilian V., *The Trouble with Tax Competition: From Practice to Theory*, 71 TAX L. REV. 311 (2018)

Flanagan, Jacqueline Laínez, *Holding U.S. Corporations Accountable: Toward a Convergence of U.S. International Tax Policy and International Human Rights*, 45 PEPP. L. REV. 685 (Apr. 2018)

Gargouri, Slim, *Singapore Strengthens Africa Tax Treaty Network: More Certainty to Boost Trade and Investment*, 29 J. INT'L TAX'N 63 (July 2018)

Goodwill, Robert C., Jr., and Janie Whiteaker-Poe, *International Taxation 101: The Revenue Proposals that Will Keep the Status Quo and a Formulary Approach that Won't*, 18 HOUS. BUS. & TAX L.J. 150 (2018)

Gupta, Ranjana, *Hybrid Entities and Double Tax Agreement Relief: India and New Zealand Approach*, 24 NZJTLP 265 (Sept. 2018)

Hansen, Robin F., *Taking More Than They Give: MNE Tax Privateering and Apple's "Ocean" Income*, 19 GERMAN L.J. 693 (July 2018)

Harms, Joshua D., *Legislative Foundation of the United States' New International Tax System*, 42 SEATTLE U. L. REV. 211 (Fall 2018)

Income Inclusion Caused by Subpart F Law Changes will not cause PTP to lose status, 129 J. TAX'N 41 (Aug. 2018)

Interim and Transitition Rules for Calculating UBTI for Separate Businesses Under TCJA, 30 TAX'N EXEMPTS 34 (Nov./Dec. 2018)

IRS Limits Use of Mandatory Transfer Pricing IDR and Instructs Examiners on Penalties in Transfer Pricing Cases, 128 J. TAX'N 40 (May 2018)

Karas, Matt, *Be Careful What You Wish For: How International Tax Coordination Could Necessitate a U.S. Patent Box*, 9 GEO. MASON J. INT'L COM. L. 211 (Spring 2018)

Kim, Young Ran (Christine), *Carried Interest and Beyond: The Nature of Private Equity Investment and Its International Tax Implications*, 37 VA. TAX REV. 421 (2018)

Kim, Sang Man and Jingho Kim, *Flags of Convenience in the Context of the OECD BEPS Package*, 49 J. MAR. L. & COM. 221 (2018)

Kleyn, Madeline M., *BEPS Project and Intangibles: Impact On IP Tax Structures*, 53 LES NOUVELLES 148 (June 2018)

Kysar, Rebecca M., *Critiquing (and Repairing) the New International Tax Regime*, 128 YALE L.J. FORUM 339 (2018)

Langbein, Stanley I., and Max R. Fuss, *The OECD/G20-BEPS-Project and the Value Creation Paradigm: Economic Reality Disemboguing into the Interpretation of the "Arm's Length" Standard*, 51 INT'L LAW 259 (2018)

Lazo, Christina M., *Adapt Globally Some Strategies for Domestic Fund Managers*, 45 EST. PLAN. 24 (Sept. 2018)

Loevy, Karin, *Railways, Ports, and Irregation: The Forgotten Regional Landscape of the Sykes-Picot Agreement*, 36 B.U. INT'L L.J. 287 (Summer 2018)

Lowell, Cym H., Mark P. Thomas, and Kristina L. Novak, *The International Provisions of the TCJA*, 45 WGL-CTAX 18 (March/April 2018)

Mararin, Raquel M., *Colorado Provides Guidance on Post-TCJA IRC Section 965 Deemed Repatriation Rules*, 28 J. MULTISTATE TAX'N 36 (Sept. 2018)

McCormick, Patrick J., *International Tax For the Growing Business*, 128 J. TAX'N 16 (June 2018)

Michalski, Katlynn, *Equalizing or Encroaching? Ireland's Place in the European Commission's Move Toward Tax Harmony*, 35 WIS. INT'L L.J. 704 (Summer 2018)

Mitchell, Andrew D. and Neha Mishra, *Data at the Docks: Modernizing International Trade Law for the Digital Economy*, 20 VAND. J. ENT. & TECH. L. 1073 (Summer 2018)

Morier, Drew, Peter Macdonald, and Alex Klyguine, *Canadian Federal Budget 2018: Overview*, 29 J. INT'L TAX'N 30 (June 2018)

Nam, Seunghyun, *Domestic Impact of the Management Process Under the OECD Anti-Bribery Convention*, 39 U. PA. J. INT'L L. 955 (Summer 2018)

Oei, Shu-Yi, *Diane Ring, Leak-Driven Law*, 65 UCLA L. REV. 532 (2018)

Oei, Shu-Yi, *The Offshore Tax Enforcement Dragnet*, 67 EMORY L.J. 655 (2018)

Offshore Voluntary Disclosure Program Ending in September, 128 J. TAX'N 04 (May 2018)

Oosterhuis, Paul and Amanda Parsons, *Destination-Based Income Taxation: Neither Principled Nor Practical?*, 71 TAX L. REV. 515 (Spring 2018)

Parnes, Alan P., Abraham Gutwein, et. al., *Challenges of TCJA to U.S. Individuals with Foreign Business Interests*, 129 J. TAX'N 06 (Nov. 2018)

Pelton, Valerie J. *JEBEL ALI: Open for Business*, 27 TRANSAT'L L. & CONTEMP. PROBS. 375 (Summer 2018)

Reed, Jeffrey S. *State Tax Impact of the Transition Tax and GITLI*, 28 J. MULTISTATE TAX'N 41 (June 2018)

Requena, Jose Angel Gomez *Smart Contracts as an Instrument to Price Intercompany Transactions at Arm's Length*, 29 J. INT'L TAX'N 58 (Aug. 2018)

Richardson-Dunkley, Judith, *Pennsylvania Issues Guidance on Repatriation Transition Tax*, 28 J. MULTISTATE TAX'N 35 (July 2018)

Sanderson, Adam T. *Overstepping Its Boundaries: The European Commission Followed the OECD's Influence But Went One Step Too Far*, 45 SYRACUSE J. INT'L L. & COM. 275 (Spring 2018)

Sawyer, Adrian *Who Cares about Tax Theory and Why?*, 24 NZJTLP 221 (Sept. 2018)

Schumacher, Aaron, Richard Levine, and Shudan Zhou, *Tax Cuts and Jobs Act: Impact on Chinese Clients' Wealth and Business Interest Planning*, 29 J. INT'L TAX'N 36 (May 2018)

Seago, W. Eugene, Kenneth Orbach, and Edward J. Schnee, *Tax Engineering the C Corporation Interest Deduction Under the TCJA*, 129 J. TAX'N 6 (Aug. 2018)

Sheppard, Hale E., *"Reasonable Cause" Defense in Nonwillful FBAR Penalty Case: Early Teachings from Jarnagin*, 29 J. INT'L TAX'N 46 (Sept. 2018)

Sheppard, Hale E., Esq., *What Constitutes a "Willful" FBAR Violation?*, 129 J. TAX'N 24 (Nov. 2018)

Sheppard, Hale E., *Alarming U.S. Tax Rules And Information-Reporting Duties For Foreign Retirement Plans: Problems And Solutions*, 129 J. TAX'N 14, 2018 WL 4802380 (October 2018)

Sheppard, Hale E., *Collecting Tax Liabilities Abroad: International Reach Of The IRS*, 29 J. INT'L TAX'N 34, 2018 WL 1518684 (February 2018)

Sheppard, Hale E., *Analysis of the "Reasonable Cause" Defense In Non-Willful FBAR Penalty Case: Teachings From Jarnagin*, 128 J. TAX'N 06, 2018 WL 1666388 (April 2018)

Silbering-Meyer, Jessica, *U.S. Transfer Pricing: BEPS Effect*, 29 J. INT'L TAX'N 48 (May 2018)

Silbering-Meyer, Jessica, *Tax Cuts and Jobs Act: A Response to BEPS*, 29 J. INT'L TAX'N 40 (Sept. 2018)

Silbering-Meyer, Jessica, *ITI: Group Financing Following U.S. Tax Reform*, 29 J. INT'L TAX'N 62 (Sept. 2018)

Spencer, David Eric, *BEPS and the Allocation of Taxing Rights (Part 4)*, 29 J. INT'L TAX'N 34 (Apr. 2018)

Stanford, Beth Anne, and Julian A. Fortuna, *International, Tax Provisions Are Already in Effect. Is Your Company Ready?*, 36 no. 5 ACC Docket 62 (July 3018)

Stein, Jacob, and Leticia Balcazar, *Inbound Taxation Changes Under the 2017 Tax Cuts and Job Act*, 129 J. TAX'N 16 (Sept. 2018)

Stephens, Rachel M., *Indiana Updates IRC Conformity and Makes Other Tax Law Changes*, 28 J. MULTISTATE TAX'N 38 (Aug. 2018)

Tian, Dr. George Yijun, *Cloud Computing and Cross-Border Transfer Pricing: Implications of Recent OECD and Australian Transfer Pricing Laws on Cloud Related Multinational Enterprises and Possible Solutions*, 44 RUTGERS COMPUTER & TECH. L.J. 33 (2018)

Wallace, Max Matthew, II, *No, You Really Don't Have to Pay: Protecting Tax Havens*, 46 GA. J. INT'L & COMP. L. 809 (Spring 2018)

Wang, Boyu, *After the European Commission Ordered Apple to Pay Back Taxes to Ireland: Ireland's Future in the New Global Tax Environment*, 25 IND. J. GLOBAL LEGAL STUD. 539 (Spring 2018)

Weissbart, Sean R., *Impact of Expanded Definition of "U.S. Shareholder" On Foreign Trust Beneficiaries*, 45 EST. PLAN. 24 (June 2018)

West, Phil, *Tax Reform Readiness: Impact on Deals, Joint Ventures, Strategic Alliances*, 29 J. INT'L TAX'N 28 (July 2018)

West, Phil, *Argentina Issues Additional Regs. on Taxation of Nonresident Investors*, 29 J. INT'L TAX'N 05 (July 2018)

West, Phil, *Repatriation Tax Ripples: Restricting Changes to Accounting Period*, 129 J. TAX'N 42 (Aug. 2018)

Wu, Tang Hang, *From WAQF, Ancestor Worship to the Rise of the Global Trust: A History of the Use of the Trust as a Vehicle for Wealth Transfer in Singapore*, 103 IOWA L. REV. 2263 (July 2018)

Yang, James G.S., Wing W. Poon, et. al., *The Important Aspects and Strategies of the TCJA*, 101 PRAC. TAX STRATEGIES 16 (July 2018)

Yang, James G.S., Victor Metallo, and Jeffrey S. Warren, *TCJA: Worldwide vs. Territorial System*, 29 J. INT'L TAX'N 30 (Aug. 2018)

Index

Titles in the **Elgar Advanced Introductions** series include:

Comparative Constitutional Law
Second Edition
Mark Tushnet

National Innovation Systems
*Cristina Chaminade, Bengt-Åke
Lundvall and Shagufta Haneef*

Ecological Economics
Matthias Ruth

Private International Law and
Procedure
Peter Hay

Freedom of Expression
Mark Tushnet

Law and Globalisation
Jaakko Husa

Regional Innovation Systems
*Bjørn T. Asheim, Arne Isaksen and
Michaela Trippl*

International Political Economy
Second Edition
Benjamin J. Cohen

International Tax Law
Second Edition
Reuven S. Avi-Yonah